WHEN GOD SPEAKS
IN
PARABLES

VOLUME 1

OTHER BOOKS BY THE AUTHOR

WHEN GOD SPEAKS

IN

PARABLES

VOLUME 1

Understanding Jesus' Parables on Obedience, Faith, and Holiness

Dami I. Olu (Ph.D.)

Dedicated to my father, who is now safe with my Father in heaven.

"The memory of the righteous is blessed, but the name of the wicked will rot." (Prov. 10:7)

CONTENTS

—

ACKNOWLEDGMENTS

My deepest appreciation to my wife, Dolapo, for her support, love, and encouragement during this period, and always.

Many thanks to my daughter, Christabel, my own heart living in a smaller body, for bringing so much joy into my life.

Thanks to my mother and my siblings. I count myself blessed to have you as my support system and co-travellers on this journey.

Thanks to my church, pastors, and friends for their support and prayers.

INTRODUCTION

C an I start by telling you a short story? There was once an old man who thought he could change the world just by sitting quietly on a tiny rocking chair—his ancient and versatile throne—and gazing at the distant jagged mountains through the begrimed window of his dinky room. Those mountains have been challenging the rustic skyline in silent defiance for as long as he could remember. They were kindred spirits, mirroring the defiance in his own dark soul.

He diligently—if one could use that word in this sense—sat and looked through the window for seven hours every day. Sunday through Saturday, no exceptions. Just seven hours; never short or more. Seven was his magic number. Little did he know that—Oh, wait. Are you … enjoying … the story already? I suppose you are. Well, that is what this book is all about: the innate power of storytelling and its ability to grip our attention, deftly injecting the message into our minds.

Whether young or old, we all love good stories. We can safely assume that long before one of the oldest surviving written works of literature, the Epic of Gilgamesh (spoiler alert: the gods are angry, and the eponymous King Gilgamesh goes on a quest to find immortality, and so on),[1] was engraved on ancient Babylonian tablets some 4,000 years ago, oral storytelling thrived in most societies of the ancient world. Even now, very few things excite children all over the world more than that ubiquitous introduction: "Once upon a time," especially when paired with the romanticized conclusion, "and they lived happily ever after." Whether chatting with a friend, reading a book, listening to a radio program, or watching a movie, storytelling is all around us.

A well-delivered story builds anticipation in us and engages our imagination as the narrative progresses and the plot reaches its crescendo. Depending on the intent and delivery, a story may end up easing our emotions or could leave us with heightened emotions that serve as a seed for further conversation, becoming a gift that keeps on giving.

Even when no one is actively telling us stories, our minds keep generating narratives throughout the day. When we are sleeping, our storytelling machine, the mind, continues its production of stories, which we often term *dreams*.

King Solomon opined that dreams come through many cares carried over from our conscious waking hours (Eccles. 5:3). Others believe dreams are divine warnings or instructions, as in the cases of

Pharaoh, Jacob, Joseph, and King Nebuchadnezzar. Some modern thinkers suggest dreams compensate for deficiencies or distortions in the conscious mind. The Swiss psychiatrist and psychoanalyst Carl Jung (1875–1961) referred to these deficiencies as the *shadow* or positive sides of our personalities that we overlook, disregard, and repress.[2] Regardless of one's explanation for the origin of dreams, almost all can agree that dreams are by nature often filled with vivid imagery, even though the flow and sequence may not always align with the familiar logic of our conscious moments.

Stories do not just influence our emotions; they also inspire us and change our perspective and behaviour. Thus, storytelling is an incredibly powerful transformative tool in the hands of skillful storytellers. While I do not come close to being one, I know someone who can be called the Master Storyteller of all time—Jesus Christ. He used captivating stories called *parables* to deliver eternal truths into the hearts of His listeners thousands of years ago. And He still does, even today.

The word *parable* is a transliteration of the Greek word *parabolē*, which literally means to throw alongside. This implies that a parable is a form of comparison, analogy, or juxtaposition. It also means to set beside, suggesting that a parable is a story set beside a reality or truth, forming a parallel system of literal and corresponding figurative meanings. We can also define a parable as a mundane, relatable story used to convey deep truths or realities.

Like other forms of storytelling, parables have an intended end and a means to achieve that end. However, it is easier to understand the means than it is to grasp the purpose. The means by which a parable achieves its end is storytelling that parallels a spiritual concept with relatable stories. Hence, we can also define parables as extended metaphors. While we cannot conclude that the parables told by Jesus are all historical, they are all relatable nonetheless. They are not some fantastic fairy tales told to excite the thrill-seeking mind.

Though some have differentiated between parables and allegories, it suffices for this conversation to say parables lay the literal story parallel to the corresponding truth, while allegories intertwine the literal and the figurative into a single tapestry of encoded truth. Thus, though parables and allegories may differ in structure, they are applied to the same end. For example, the allegory of the good shepherd shares a similar theme with the parable of the lost sheep—that is, God cares for His sheep, whether they are safe in the pen or are lost in the field.

Some believe that a major difference between a parable and an allegory is that a parable teaches only one spiritual truth, while an allegory contains several elements, each representing a specific idea. I do not believe there are scriptural limitations on the number of lessons one can learn from a single parable. Though every parable told by Jesus Christ has a central theme, we can glean several lessons from each. The aim of this work is to shed light on the lessons embedded in each parable. However, the goal is not to dig so deeply into them that we arrive at conclusions other that what the Holy Spirit intends for us. It is my firm belief that since the Holy Spirit is the Author of the Bible, He is also its best interpreter. Consequently, the task of dividing the truth of God's Word should be done under the influence of the Holy Spirit.

In line with the above recommendation, I constantly sought the guidance of the Holy Spirit while preparing this work—to avoid falling into the error of overextending the parables. The aim of this study is not to shock or intrigue the reader with never-heard-before truths. Such a mindset often leads to abuse of Scriptures. Rather, this work seeks to unveil the hidden gems that God intends for us to find through diligent study. We should seek knowledge not just for its sake, but for the transformation of our lives as we live in obedience to God's Word. For the Bible says:

> The secret things belong to the LORD our God, but those things which are revealed belong to us and to our children forever, that we may do all the words of this law. (Deut. 29:29)

If reading this work moves you, even to a small degree, closer to God, then my work here is done, and all the glory belongs to God!

Chapter 1

WHY PARABLES?

෨෨෨෨෨෨෨෨෨෨

During His time here on earth, Jesus used a perfect blend of direct messaging, parables, allegories, and, of course, His exemplary living to convey His messages. For example, the oft quoted Sermon on the Mount (Matt. 5–7) contains a mix of these elements. Yet there appears to be something unique about Jesus' use of parables to convey deep truths to His audiences. So why did He use parables at all? Identifying the reasons Jesus used parables instead of direct messaging is an interesting subject, which we will discuss in this chapter.

Parables, like other forms of storytelling, have many advantages over direct messaging. We discuss next some of these advantages as a precursor to our in-depth analysis of the parables of Jesus Christ.

ADVANTAGES OF STORYTELLING

Stories grip our attention and break the monotony. Have you ever caught yourself dozing off or absent-minded during a sermon, until the preacher said, "I remember a story I heard years ago"? At that point, it probably felt like you just regained consciousness, and by looking around at the other congregants, you could tell you were not alone. You were all indeed fellows on the same ship. Even if you were paying attention before the story, it still drew you in. Effective use of a story by a preacher ensures that whenever the listeners remember the story, whatever the memory trigger may be, their minds link it back to the truth to which it was anchored. However, caution is required so that the story does not steal the show and become its own end.

Stories can facilitate objectivity. A story can easily break through our tendency to get defensive when confronted directly by some truth. We see no need to become defensive, as the story affords us the opportunity to stand aside as the unbiased judge of the characters in it. Thus, stories help to smuggle or sneak the truth past our guarded hearts. For example, King David had taken and slept with Uriah's only wife, Bathsheba. Uriah the Hittite was one of David's soldiers and was deeply loyal to him and Israel. Yet David took his wife while he was on the battlefront for his king and country. As if that weren't awful enough, David orchestrated Uriah's death by commanding that he be placed where the battle was fiercest. Clearly, the king was in the wrong; he had committed a grievous sin—yet he seemed oblivious to it, just like we often have blind spots for our own sins. The pressing question was: Who was going to confront and tell the king that he was wrong? God sent Prophet Nathan to do just that. That was a dangerous task for the prophet!

Kings, in those days, had almost absolute power over matters of life and death, and in a moment of rage or perceived insubordination could decree instant death on the unfortunate offender. To confront the king about his sin seemed suicidal, especially against the backdrop of David's immediate predecessor, King Saul, who had murdered many priests for several contrived offences.

Wise Prophet Nathan employed storytelling to admonish the king—and, in this case, storytelling served as a lifesaver. Had the prophet confronted and admonished the king directly, he could have become defensive and angry. But the use of a story put him at ease as an objective judge of the character of the wealthy evil man who had many sheep but still covetously took the only sheep of his poor neighbour. When the prophet finally clarified that the king was the evil man in the story, it was too late for him to rescind his unintended objectivity. He humbled himself and repented.

Stories have staying power in the mind. While it is highly unlikely that you can recall verbatim any of the sermons you heard twenty or thirty years ago, you are more likely to easily recall the stories you heard during the same period, whether told or sung. Similarly, while many Christians cannot correctly quote more than a couple of Bible verses, many can easily recite the popular parables in the Bible. For instance, some non-Christians, who cannot quote even a single Bible verse, know the parable of the prodigal son, if only in part. Children may leave home and may not remember the exact words of their parents, but the stories stay with them.

I would venture to suggest at this juncture that parents and teachers should make the most of storytelling in instructing their children or wards. They should not just prepare sermons for the children, but also create short stories to which they can anchor the sermons. Jesus Christ is, of course, the Master Storyteller. His stories are short and simple enough to not distract from the message. When stories get too long and complicated, they become confusing and difficult to remember. Further, they risk becoming an end in themselves, rather than a means to an end. The end is always the spiritual truth to be revealed. The maxim is: Encode it in a story, and the memory lingers.

Stories inform our philosophy and morality. It is often difficult to form a cohesive and comprehensive philosophy based on momentary or sporadic experiences. A more complete picture affords us the resources with which we can develop a robust and comprehensive philosophy. Stories provide us with this big picture. Just as it is difficult to draw the landscape of a field while standing right in the middle of it, it is difficult to develop good philosophy or morality on the spur of the moment. We may need to be taken out and above the landscape to get a vantage point that provides a clearer and more complete view.

We meet people at specific points in their lives, and it is almost impossible to form a coherent philosophy or morality based on the incomplete information we get at those points in time. For instance, if some of your acquaintances regularly smoke packs of cigarettes a day, the present information may paint them as cool guys just having fun. However, your view may change as time reveals the consequences of their prolonged chain-smoking habit.

> *Children may leave home and may not remember the exact words of their parents, but the stories stay with them.*

If we suppose, for the sake of argument, that there is no existing body of knowledge on the dangers of smoking cigarettes, what becomes of your acquaintances in the next thirty to forty years is information which is not available to you right now but is required to form a coherent philosophy about smoking cigarettes. Stories can compress an entire lifetime into a few lines or minutes, allowing us to see the entire picture at once and correspondingly inform our philosophy or morality. Stories can serve as reality compressed in time. In this sense, history is essentially compressed stories of past events and people.

Stories can help forge and sustain relationships. Many people enjoy the company of an excellent storyteller. Listeners are often delighted by good stories, even when they know some or all the stories are nothing more than a tall tale. Our society rewards many professional storytellers—movie stars, authors, comedians, skit-makers, etc.—with fame, wealth, and much more. Some storytellers are even entrusted with power, be it political or ecclesiastical. Stories have the potential to boost feelings such as love, empathy, judgment, and justice in us. When we hear a well-delivered story, we often get emotionally involved with it, even to the point of empathy. In other words, a good story places us in it.

Stories are units of cultural transmission. Stories are often used to distil complex social relationships and transmit knowledge of social norms (laws, mores, taboos, and folkways) from one generation to the next. They are often used to instil mores and good behaviours. Using stories, a particular group may immortalize past conflicts or cooperations with another group, serving as a reminder or caution to generations yet unborn.

Stories are used to explain the world around us. Long before the advent of the scientific method and psychoanalysis, diverse societies crafted stories to explain the origin and nature of the external world: the weather; the sun; moon; stars; humans; animals; rivers; and the unseen dynamics of life, such as destiny, morality, fate, and death. In this context, stories often take on a religious fervour as most of these explanatory stories ultimately end up with gods as originators or overseers of various aspects of the world and life in general.

Even with science, storytelling can make a vast difference in how students engage with a subject. A talented scientist does not necessarily make an excellent science teacher. It takes the combination of the knowledge of science and the art of storytelling to make an excellent science teacher who can distil knowledge in a manner that helps students appreciate the beauty of science and fall in love with it. The same applies to other academic or vocational disciplines.

Stories can be used to subjugate, vilify, or whitewash events and people. A popular quote says, "History is written by the victors." What if most of what we know today as history is a carefully crafted narrative by the victors to paint themselves in a good light? After all, the losers are either dead or too weak to tell their own side of the story. A murderer in a bygone era may be currently celebrated as the saviour, based on what story has been crafted, disseminated, and widely accepted as settled history. The question remains: Is history set in stone or is it fluid?

Storytelling is an invitation to come along on a creative journey. An excellent storyteller invites the listeners not just to listen passively, but to come along on a journey of creativity. If the images created in the mind of each listener were to be projected on a screen, it would be interesting to see the different pictures formed and the artistic liberties taken by each listener as they make the story their own. Same story, but different depth of understanding, imagination, and interpretation. For example, if a story about a slave is being narrated, the listeners have some degree of liberty to imagine the slave as they deem fit, without compromising the spirit of the story.

The results will vary based on several factors, such as the existing knowledge of the listener about slavery and its attendant hardship. Other relevant factors include the social class, religious beliefs, and the political leanings of the listener. Slaves listening to the story may paint a representative picture of the slave in their hearts, but the expected intensity of accompanying emotions may be surprisingly absent. It is a case of blissful ignorance of how dire their current condition is.

> When we hear a well-delivered story, we often get emotionally involved with it, even to the point of empathy. In other words, a good story places us in it.

In contrast, freemen or former slaves listening to the same story have the benefit of hindsight and contrast to appreciate, to a fuller extent, the terrible condition of the slave in the story. This may explain why a wealthy tourist to a poor country may be acutely aware of the unlivable conditions of the citizens of the country and yet marvel at their happiness despite all their suffering.

When living in a terrible condition for an extended period, the mind soon adapts by using several survival mechanisms, such as downplaying the awfulness of the condition, accepting it as fate, or even weaving a theological narrative around it—while hoping for a better day. However, once out of the condition, there is no more need for the band-aid. The former sufferer can now, with brutal honesty, criticize the situation, often in the most severe manner possible.

WHY DID JESUS SPEAK IN PARABLES?

Jesus Christ used parables to encode truths about the kingdom of heaven. "In fact, in His public ministry He never taught without using parables" (Mark 4:34 New Living Translation). He deliberately spoke in parables to screen out listeners with ulterior motives. Some came to set a trap for Him with their sweet talks and seemingly harmless questions. About this set of people, the Gospel of Matthew reports:

"Then the Pharisees went and plotted how they might entangle Him in His talk" (Matt. 22:15).

Some wanted to use Him to gain earthly possessions and feed their greed (Luke 12:13). Others came to Him because of the miracles or food they could get from Him (John 6:26). Probably only a few people came to Him to learn of Him and for the salvation of their souls. In response to these varieties of intentions, Jesus encoded His public teachings in parables. People who had selfish intentions and were only interested in personal gain rarely understood the parables and didn't try to understand them, as their focus was on fulfilling their own selfish desires.

In a fortunate contrast, those who were serious enough about knowing more of Him went back to seek His help with understanding the parables (Mark 4:34). They saw the parables as an invitation to a deeper talk and walk with Christ. Thus, Jesus used parables as a sifter to separate the intentional and genuine seekers from the ones with selfish agendas. The Gospel of Mark puts it this way:

> So that "seeing they may see and not perceive, and hearing they may hear and not understand; lest they should turn, and their sins be forgiven them." (Mark. 4:12)

Even when these selfish seekers understood Jesus' parables, they got offended, mocked, and sought to kill Him, rather than repent of their sins (Luke 16:14). It is therefore important as we approach this study to come with a humble heart, for God resists the proud and gives grace to the humble (James 4:6). Those who approach God with humility value His Word so much that they take it to heart, seek further insight, and allow it to transform them. More will be given to those who have been faithful with the little they are currently managing.

In contrast, those who approach God with pride and ulterior motives do not profit by the Word. They would rather analyze, criticize, and judge the Word than obey it. For these people, fewer revelations of the Word are released in the future. Jesus' words to them are:

> For whoever has, to him more will be given, and he will have abundance; but whoever does not have, even what he has will be taken away from him. Therefore, I speak to them in parables. (Matt. 13:12–13)

If we close our eyes to the truth already revealed to us, additional truths will not be released. We must appreciate and make profit with what we already have. Otherwise, even the truth we think we know may slip away from us. Those who open their hearts to the truth will receive the revelation of more truths. As we receive His grace, the parables open up and reveal their hidden gems to us. To the selfish seekers, the parables may mean nothing more than sweet stories, for

> the natural man does not receive the things of the Spirit of God, for they are foolishness to him; nor can he know them, because they are spiritually discerned. (1 Cor. 2:14)

HOW MANY PARABLES?

The number of parables varies based on how one defines a parable. For example, some scholars classify the story of the rich man and Lazarus as a parable, while others do not. Further, some of the stories are classified as allegories, rather than parables. There appears to be a consensus that the synoptic Gospels (Matthew, Mark, and Luke) contain all the parables, while the Gospel of John is distinct, as it does not contain any parable. John used allegories instead.

Based on the differences in definition, the parables could number anywhere from thirty to over fifty. This work includes only stories that were either identified explicitly as parables in the Scriptures or are generally agreed upon by Bible scholars to be such. In total, about thirty parables are discussed in this work—split evenly over three volumes.

An excellent storyteller invites the listeners not just to listen passively, but to come along on a journey of creativity.

We should be more concerned about the lessons God wants us to learn from the parables than paying undue attention to pinning down their exact number. After all, the most important thing about the parables, and indeed all the teachings of Jesus, is to understand and live by them.

Although Jesus used parables extensively during His earthly ministry, the authors of the Gospels did not record them to the same extent. The parables as recorded in the synoptic Gospels share a lot of similarities, but there are some differences in some instances. This is not a cause for concern, as the key themes of the parables are preserved. These minor differences are probably due to differences in style and emphasis by the individual authors.

HIDDEN BUT REVEALED TO BABES

Stories are powerful tools for conveying information, eliciting emotions, and transforming mindsets and behaviours. The parables told by Jesus Christ form the focus of this work. The goal of the parables is to reveal to us kingdom mysteries and transform our lives through our encounter with these truths. After all, what is the use of the truth we claim to know but has failed to set us free?

The true test of whether we know the truth is if we have been liberated by it. We do not truly know until we are free. It is therefore important that we do not take these parables with levity. Jesus revealed the inestimable worth of the gems concealed in His teachings when He said,

> I thank You, Father, Lord of heaven and earth, that You have hidden these things from the wise and the prudent and have revealed them to babes. (Matt. 11:25)

HOW SHOULD WE ENGAGE THE PARABLES?

Whether we encounter these parables in private or public, it is important that we understand and acknowledge that we are not just passive hearers. We interact with the parables. We influence them as much as they influence us; it is a two-way coupling effect. Our experiences, ideologies, and current state of mind may colour the parables. Confirmation bias also applies to them. We have the tendency to cherry-pick and interpret them in a manner that confirms and supports our prior beliefs, ideologies, or values.

Thus, Jesus used parables as a sifter to separate the intentional and genuine seekers from the ones with selfish agendas.

A rich man once dreamed he died. Panic-stricken, he ran to his shaman for help. The shaman told him the remedy was to avoid setting his sight on any colour, except green. The rich man had his servants paint every object in his house and surroundings green. There was a slight problem though: the sky. It's not ... that ... green, and it's a bit out of reach. How would he get rid of this non-green sky? He hid away in his well-curtained mansion until he became frustrated and bored to tears. Finally, he went back to the shaman and vented his frustration. The shaman led him to the door and asked him to close his eyes. After a few seconds, he asked him to open them again. On opening his eyes, the rich man found himself looking directly at the sky—and it was all green! Did a miracle just happen? No. The shaman simply placed a pair of green-tinted glasses over his eyes.

> *The true test of whether we know the truth is if we have been liberated by it. We do not truly know until we are free.*

Similarly, how we perceive the world is not just about how the world is, but also how we, the observers, are. Different people can view the same parable through different tinted glasses—the tint of pride, social justice, different -*isms*, political beliefs, etc. The Bible clearly tells us that "prophecy never came by the will of man, but holy men of God spoke as they were moved by the Holy Spirit" (2 Pet. 1:21). Thus, to ensure we stay true to the original intents of the parables, it will bode well for us to ask for the Author's help whenever we engage with the parables.

One of the greatest benefits of the Bible is that the Author can be present with every reader or listener, if invited. Since the parables, like any story, can easily be influenced by the biases of the reader or listener, we should invite the Holy Spirit as our guide while reading this work. We should compare Scriptures with Scriptures to confirm the veracity of the interpretations provided and be careful not to extend the parables beyond their original intents. *Scriptura sacra sui ipsius interpres* (sacred Scripture is its own interpreter).

> *One of the greatest benefits of the Bible is that the Author can be present with every reader or listener, if invited.*

As a parable may contain multiple lessons peripheral to its central theme, the aim of this work is not to decipher all the lessons in each parable. Making such a claim is neither realistic nor wise. In the belief that we know in part (1 Cor. 13:9), the aim of this work is to trust God to reveal some of the relevant lessons to us as we prayerfully study the parables. God has the prerogative to reveal deeper insights into His Word progressively. However, as a rule and guardrail, no lesson gleaned from any of Jesus' parables should contradict the central theme of the parable or established truths revealed in other parts of the Bible. All the lessons, wherever and whenever revealed, must complement, not contradict, themselves or the Word of God. "For God is not the author of confusion but of peace, as in all the churches of the saints" (1 Cor. 14:33).

Can you please take a minute to pray for the guidance of the Holy Spirit as you read along? Happy reading!

Chapter 2

THE WISE AND
FOOLISH BUILDERS

ৡ৽ৡ৽ৡ৽ৡ৽ৡ৽ৡ৽ৡ৽ৡ৽ৡ৽

Therefore, whoever hears these sayings of Mine, and does them, I will liken him to a wise man who built his house on the rock: and the rain descended, the floods came, and the winds blew and beat on that house; and it did not fall, for it was founded on the rock. But everyone who hears these sayings of Mine, and does not do them, will be like a foolish man who built his house on the sand: and the rain descended, the floods came, and the winds blew and beat on that house; and it fell. And great was its fall.

MATTHEW 7:24–27

In the verses preceding this parable (vv. 15–23), Jesus had just cautioned us against two major pitfalls: being fooled by wolves in sheep's clothing and being lawless in our relationship with Him. Both warnings point to the fact that things are not always what they appear to be. The parable begins with the word *Therefore*, indicating that it is logically and spiritually built on the preceding cautionary notes.

The litmus test to determine who a person really is cannot be their mere profession. It is their fruit. "You will know them by their fruits" (Matt. 7:16). It is possible to call Jesus, "Lord, Lord" but not enter His kingdom. To enter His kingdom, we must bear good fruit, and we bear good fruit when we do the will of our Father in heaven as revealed in His Word. Thus, Jesus established an unbreakable link between entering His kingdom and obeying His Word. The one who does not obey His Word *will not* enter His kingdom.

We do not become fruitful by merely professing that we know, believe, or love God. After all, Christians are not the only *believers* in

God. Satan and his hosts are also firm believers in God. The Epistle of James says, "You believe that there is one God. You do well. Even the demons believe—and tremble!" (James 2:19). Demons believe in God, but their belief does not translate to their salvation because they do not obey His Word. They are rebels. This shows that mere profession or belief is not sufficient for salvation.

Jesus did not die for the angels; He died for humanity. Yet the angels in heaven are not doomed. Why? Because they continuously obey God. In contrast, the angels who sided with the devil rebelled against God, disobeyed Him, and are eternally doomed. This shows that the requirement of obedience to God transcends humanity. Even the heavenly hosts are expected to obey the sovereignty of God. To do otherwise is to invite eternal damnation.

We know we cannot bear fruit just by mere profession or belief. But that's not all. Neither do we bear fruit by engaging in several activities in the church. In fact, we do not bear fruit by prophesying, casting out demons, or performing many wonders—even using Jesus' name. Though these are what we often deem the hallmarks of great and celebrated men and women of God, Jesus said these powerful actions, in and of themselves, do not amount to bearing good fruit.

To bear good fruit, we must obey His Word. The manifestation of the gifts of the Spirit is not a sign of fruitfulness, per se. How we honour the man who casts out demons more than the one who simply obeys the commandments of God! It's not that the two are mutually exclusive or designed by God to be so; however, we often place a lot of value on power demonstrations in the church, but at the expense of fruit. How we live our lives and spend our time and resources are better indicators of our spiritual health than anything we profess or miracles performed through our hands.

ALL THAT GLITTERS IS NOT GOLD

Many choose marriage partners based on charisma, talents, beauty, wealth, and manifested spiritual gifts. They *friendzone* people who obey the Word of God and are therefore fruitful—that is, they have the fruit of the Spirit evident in their lives. Once in the marriage, these people complain about issues of which they were the architects.

THE WISE AND FOOLISH BUILDERS

How much sorrow they could have spared themselves, if only they had heeded the warning Jesus is giving us here!

Although recognized as a spiritual giant in the church here on earth, one may not be recognized in heaven. Jesus said, "I never knew you; depart from Me, you who practice lawlessness" (Matt. 7:23). We cannot serve God just any way we please. God's building must be built according to His pattern.

Many preachers have succumbed to their emotions in ministry. They preach their feelings, eloquently and passionately, rather than the Word of God. They may grace our TV screens and sell millions of books, yet in the register of heaven, their names may be missing. Jesus may not know them. Unfortunately, many believers choose their preachers based solely on charisma, eloquence, looks, dress sense, spiritual gifts, and frankly, anything, except demonstrable obedience to the Word of God.

Some preachers live in public defiance of God's revealed truth in His Word, and yet people follow them. Jesus called such preachers *lawless*. And the people who follow them blindly, or for some other wrong reasons, are contributing to the lawlessness in the church, with a resultant spill over to the larger world.

LAWLESSNESS IN THE CHURCH

This lawlessness is not endemic to the pulpit; even the pew is affected. I once met a sister who had little to no regard for her husband. They were both Christians, but she felt she had advanced so much ahead of him spiritually that she lost all respect for him. Without informing or discussing with him, she would embark on prolonged fasts and sexual abstinence. She went on mission trips for days, notifying him only via notes. Convinced she was on fire for the Lord, she disregarded any advice or correction.

When I asked her if her actions and attitudes were in line with the Scriptures concerning marriage, she seemed to know all the relevant Scriptures but simply disregarded them because she felt she was on fire for God and no *demons* from the pit of hell could stand in her way. In her mind, her salvation was solely between her and her God, and she owed her husband no explanation. Although versed in the knowledge of Biblical injunctions concerning family relations, she placed her feelings (often misnamed *convictions*) above the Word of God. She placed her personal revelations above the revealed truth in the Word. She was figuratively and literally calling Jesus "Lord, Lord," yet she kept refusing to obey His commandments.

In a similar manner, a man once living in North America dabbled in Eastern mysticism, abandoned his family—wife and young children— and left for India because he had what he termed a *spiritual awakening*. He appeared genuinely surprised that his wife would not immediately jump on the plane with him as he set out on his *missionary* journey. He thought his family was an obstacle to his relationship with God, and he decided to leave them behind. Like most lawless people, he chose to place his private revelations or encounters above the revealed Word of God, which is forever settled in heaven. Amen.

Some Christians have been members of their local assemblies for years, yet they refuse to acknowledge or submit to any spiritual authority. They do this in several ways, including by refusing to join any group or department that would require them to be accountable or submissive to authority. Some feature in their assemblies as permanent *guest ministers*, strolling in and out whenever and however they please. Others choose activities solely on the freedom to do as they please and quit whenever they like. In some cases, some believers accuse their brethren and leaders of hypocrisy as a pretext for not submitting to authority. Some simply go down the familiar but dreadful route of procrastination, telling themselves they would get involved when the time is right—except it's been ten years already and counting.

> *How we honour the man who casts out demons more than the one who simply obeys the commandments of God!*

While online services have their place, we should be careful not to abuse them in our bid to avoid submission to spiritual authority in our local assemblies. Online services rarely have the structure to ensure accountability or discipleship, which are both necessary for our spiritual growth and the building of a solid foundation for our lives.

One of the primary causes of the Fall was the desire of our first parents to be independent of any authority, including God's. They wanted to be in control, becoming the gods of their own lives (Gen. 3:5–6). Many professing believers behave in the same manner. Their desire is to do as they please, whenever they please, and however they please. They reserve the right to disengage without warning or accountability to anyone, be it in the church or in their family. They do *good*, but only when they choose to, not at the command of God. While they may not admit to it, they are operating under a rebellious and lawless spirit.

It's in the light of the foregoing discussion that Jesus told the parable of the wise and foolish builders. How foolish would one be to labour for many years on earth while heaven recognizes neither the person nor the labour? Hence, Jesus gives us the blueprint for building our eternal destinies in a manner that will be pleasing to God.

PARTS OF A BUILDING

A building can be divided into two parts: the substructure (foundation) and the superstructure (typically above ground level). For this work, we will consider two types of foundations: shallow and deep.

The choice of a foundation depends on the soil condition and the load the foundation is expected to bear during its life. As the name implies, shallow foundations are placed close to the soil surface (often within 2 m below the surface), and their depth is typically less than their width. In contrast, deep foundations typically have a depth greater than their width, and they go much deeper into the soil. Deep foundations are used where there are weak soils near the surface or when the loads are very high, such as with large skyscrapers.

Foundations provide stability—vertical and lateral—for structures. A well-laid foundation helps to distribute the load from the superstructure to the underlying soil evenly. A weak foundation or voids in foundations can compromise the structural integrity of a building. Ignoring known foundation issues can cause a lot of structural, financial, legal, environmental, safety, and emotional woes. If there is ever an occasion where the maxim "a stitch in time saves nine" is pertinent, it is in the laying of foundations. It costs less effort, time, and money to lay a foundation properly than to repair a faulty one after the superstructure has been placed on it.

Superstructure comprises structural elements (columns, beams, slabs, etc.) and non-load-bearing elements (ornaments, claddings, etc.) that are readily seen, accessible, and often attractive by design.

In contrast, foundations are rarely designed to be attractive, as they are usually concealed from sight. We often judge the worth of two adjacent buildings solely by their superstructures. We rarely say, "Look! What a beautiful foundation!" The features that people readily admire in buildings often have very little to do with safety and stability. There may be so much to admire about a building's superstructure that no one cares about the condition of its foundation—until issues arise. But by then, it is often too late.

WHY ARE FOUNDATIONS SO IMPORTANT?

Why do we need a solid foundation? Because the rain will descend, the flood will come, and the winds will blow and beat against our house. It's not a matter of if; it is a matter of when. It is as certain as life itself. No amount of positive thinking or prophetic declarations will prevent the rain, storm, and winds from beating against our house. Trials, temptations, persecutions, disappointments, and pains are some storms of life that will pound our dwelling.

As the rain beats vertically on the house, the flood moves laterally against it, and the winds try to rip it apart, roof and all. At this point, gifts, talents, fame, and money may be of little or no avail. It's the foundation that is built on prior and continuous obedience to God's Word that will keep our house standing firm. If we have a solid foundation, we may still hear the impact, whistling, and howling of the rain, storm, and ferocious winds, but we will be safely tucked away in the house, hidden away from harm. It's not the intensity of trials that destroys a soul; failure is often due to the poor quality of the soul's foundation. "If you faint in the day of adversity, your strength is small" (Prov. 24:10).

> They do good, but only when they choose to, not at the command of God. While they may not admit to it, they are operating under a rebellious and lawless spirit.

Everyone on earth is a builder. You have been building your house all your life. The house you build determines your eternal destiny, and the foundation upon which you build determines the fate of your house. The structural engineer designs the foundation after estimating all the loads—both live and dead loads—that the foundation is expected to support throughout its life. In a similar manner, God designs our foundation based on the loads it is expected to bear. That's another reason it's foolishness to compare ourselves with others, even within the body of Christ. A foundation for a two-storey building may not require as much labour, effort, and material as one intended to support a skyscraper. While the skyscraper is still in the foundation-building stage, the entire two-storey building might have already been finished. This can lead to frustration and resentment when we wonder why things seem to work for others, but not for us.

If it seems like all your effort is not yielding corresponding results, could it be that your foundation is being dug just a little deeper? Could it be that God has a bigger plan and purpose for your life and is, therefore, taking more time to work on your foundation? That it is not readily apparent does not mean it is a waste. The fact that it is hidden doesn't make it nonexistent. Patience is a key ingredient in the making of a solid, long-lasting foundation.

What if we run out of patience and choose to build quickly on our incomplete foundation? Many young ministers have prematurely branched out to form their own ministries because they felt they were neither achieving the level of success they desired nor receiving the attention and accolades they deserved. Sadly, many of such dynamic and eager ministers have crash-landed when stability mattered most.

I remember the story of a young minister I once knew. While working under a senior minister, he felt he deserved more in terms of respect, fame, and remuneration. I'm unsure if his perception matched his actual circumstances though. He communicated his grievances to his leader and stated his readiness to move on. All attempts to persuade him to reconcile with his leader proved abortive. He left, and we missed him because he was such a lovely gentleman.

It was a rude shock when we heard of his demise only a few months afterward. He had founded a ministry that involved performing exorcism, and during a session, the possessed person was instantly healed of a particular disease. However, according to reports, as soon as the young minister returned home, he discovered that he had contracted the disease he prayed against. He was suffering from the disease he just prayed against! He died within a few days. Strangely, the disease was not a communicable one.

The news of his rapid deterioration and death shocked many people, and they spawned several theories to explain the sudden tragedy. The most prominent theory was that he was attacked spiritually during the exorcism. Yet prior to launching out on his own, he had successfully performed several exorcisms under the tutelage of the senior minister, his former leader. Could it be that the assignment he took upon himself was bigger than his spiritual foundation or capacity? We may never know, but it's important to always wait to get the green light from God before we embark on any mission. Presumption can be fatal.

We live in a time where self-promotion is relatively easy, enticing, and *empowering*. With our heads filled with strategies and our fingers set on our social media handles, we may be tempted to launch out before God releases us. Gaining many followers on social media is not a stamp of God's approval. We should wait on Him until He completes, tests, thoroughly vets, and approves our foundation before we set out to build on it. Do not rush ahead of God's timing. If the sun rises before its due time, it may set when its light and warmth are needed the most. "To everything there is a season, a time for every purpose under heaven" (Eccles. 3:1).

> *It's not the intensity of trials that destroys a soul; failure is often due to the poor quality of the soul's foundation.*

THE FOOLISH BUILDER

The foolish builder, whom we can also call the *apparent Christian*, prioritizes the superstructure over the foundation—that is, he is more concerned about making his house appear more attractive than fit for purpose. He doesn't place much value on foundation and sees it as an unnecessary waste of space and time. Rather than focus on digging deep to lay his foundation, the foolish builder focuses on putting up an imposing edifice for show.

He is impatient and always eager to move on to the next *big thing*. He wants instant rewards in terms of attention, money, success, and status. The only *truth* he loves is the one that does not cause him discomfort or challenge his lifestyle. He is an *excitement junkie*, always moving from one church to another in search of a *spiritual high*.

He chooses excitement over diligence, glamour over depth, and appearance over substance. His priority lies in the aesthetic appeal of his house rather than its functionality and durability. He refuses to take ownership of his spiritual and character development. He builds his life on *his truth* and not on *the Truth*. He fails to understand that everything (including philosophies, arguments, ideas, principles, and world views) besides Christ is sinking sand.

The foolish builder lacks discipline. He values immediate pleasure over delayed gratification. He desires God's comfort but resents His rod and staff of correction (Psa. 23:4). When in trouble, he runs from pillar to post seeking immediate relief, but he is neither ready to make amends to his ways nor remove the root cause of his problems: his perpetual disobedience to God's will. He doesn't understand that a foundation should be designed to withstand a load greater than what it endures during the building process. There may be no storm, flood, or winds during construction,

> *Everyone on earth is a builder. You have been building your house all your life. The house you build determines your eternal destiny ...*

but sure enough, they soon arrive. The foolish builder builds quickly, not considering the coming storm. His reasoning is: "If there were issues with my house, they would have been apparent during construction." He confuses God's patience—intended for his repentance—with His approval of his lifestyle.

Military experts believe one cannot build an army on the fly. In fact, they see the so-called *peacetime* as merely an interlude between wars and an opportunity to prepare for war. Little wonder nations keep spending heavily on their militaries, even during peacetime. They understand that once war starts, it is often too late to start building an army from scratch.

That your foundation (or lack of it) seems to serve you well now does not mean it will serve you well during a storm. The storm is the true test of a foundation. Many believers appear robust on a good day. They pray fervently, engage in several activities in the church, fast along with the brethren, and, from all indications, appear to be doing well—until the storms of life hit them. They crash in a sudden and devastating manner.

Both the wise and foolish builders rested confidently in their houses until the storm came. Before the storm is the best time to prepare for a storm, not when already in it. We often wait until things go awry before we seek God. The foolish builder's house collapsed *in* the storm when he needed it the most. The house fell when it was too late and dangerous to build another one.

We all love the comfort of a solid house, but are we willing to labour on building a good foundation? Let's not be like the foolish builder who had misplaced confidence in his beautiful house. His brash confidence was his ruin. About him, the Bible says,

> Their confidence hangs by a thread. They are leaning on a spider's web. They cling to their home for security, but it won't last. They try to hold it tight, but it will not endure. (Job 8:14–15 NLT)

THE WISE BUILDER

The wise builder places a premium on his foundation and takes it seriously. Before laying it, he digs out all worldly achievements, wealth, education, career, and talents. He counts them as garbage (Phil. 3:8), and he keeps digging until he reaches the rock. He cooperates with God as He helps to remove the debris from his land. He understands that God in His mercy has provided a tested and trusted rock on which he can build his house—Jesus Christ is the rock. Hear what the book of Isaiah says about that rock:

> Therefore, thus saith the Lord God, behold, I lay in Zion for a foundation a stone, a tried stone, a precious corner stone, a sure foundation: he that believeth shall not make haste. (Isa. 28:16 King James Version)

You can't make haste when building on this foundation as it takes painstaking diligence to build upon it. With great care, the wise builder meticulously follows the construction manuals as he builds on the rock. He is willing to put in the effort and sacrifice to diligently seek the Lord. He understands that constructing his house is a full-time job, not merely a side hustle. He invests his time in discovering, internalizing, and adhering to the instructions provided in the Bible.

The wise builder knows that all other ground is sinking sand. "For other foundation can no man lay than that is laid, which is Jesus Christ" (1 Cor. 3:11 KJV). He reasons that if the rock can sustain the weight of the entire universe, it can sustain the weight of his life (Heb. 1:3). Christ is the only rock on which we can build in a manner that pleases the Father and is guaranteed to last, and obedience is the only way to Christ. Concerning this rock, the book of Hebrews says, "And having been perfected, He became the Author of eternal salvation to all who obey Him" (Heb. 5:9).

The wise builder loves the truth, even if it makes him uncomfortable. He understands that the veracity of the truth is not dependent on the immediate comfort it affords. It's not lost on him that the truth that will set him free may first make him uncomfortable. Only when the Lord deems his inner light sufficient does he step into the limelight. He knows that if the light shining on him is stronger than the light within him, he may collapse under the strain. He understands the balance of taking root downward and bearing fruit upward (2 Kings 19:30).

> *Do not rush ahead of God's timing. If the sun rises before its due time, it may set when its light and warmth are needed the most.*

Before striving for new heights, he values anchoring himself in the revealed truth. His focus is on building with the storm in mind, not just for show.

So as not to mistake God's patience for an endorsement of his lifestyle, he continually seeks God's face to know the true state of his foundation. He leaves nothing to chance as he takes responsibility for his spiritual well-being and character growth. In return, his house provides him with a secure shelter in the time of storm.

One may build a grand edifice on a weak foundation; however, the building will not last. Let us therefore build our lives on God's eternal truth, not on worldly philosophies, ideologies, and our feelings. Like the wise builder, let's dig deep until we get to the truth, and then build on it. The book of Proverbs says, "Buy the truth and sell it not" (Prov. 23:23).

Talents, eloquence, power demonstrations, and emotions may enrich our experience during worship services, but they do not, by themselves, indicate the soundness of our foundation. It is obedience to the Author of our salvation that strengthens our foundation. His teachings are a stronger foundation for living than the best ideology or philosophy the world can offer (see Table 1).

Table 1: Different Foundations: A Brief Comparison of the Christian Faith and Post-modernism

Christian Faith	Post-modernism
• There is an objective and natural reality. "In the beginning God created the heavens and the earth" (Gen. 1:1). Human nature is real. God made humans in His image and likeness (Gen. 1:27).	• There is no objective natural reality. What exists is a socially accepted reality, which is a conceptual construct, an artifact of scientific practice and language.
• There are absolute truths, as established in the Word of God. Jesus is the way, the truth, and the life (John 14:6). The truth can be known. You will know the truth, and the truth will set you free (John 8:32). The truth is independent of human consensus. Forever, O Lord, Your Word is settled in heaven (Psa. 119:89).	• Truth is relative. The so-called truths have no validity beyond their relative subjective values which are largely based on perception. Advocates radical skepticism and relativism. Truth is simply a product of consensus values.
• Teaches exclusivity of Jesus Christ as the only way to the Father. "No one comes to the Father except through Me" (John 14:6).	• Advocates polyvocality, which supports the existence of multiple, legitimate versions of truths, all based on individual perspectives and experiences. In religious context, many roads lead to God.
• Since there are absolute, objective truths, deviation from them is termed sin.	• The question of sin is moot as there is no objective truth.

Though Job was battered on every side by the storms of life, he stood firm to the end because of his unshakeable foundation in God and His Word. We can say the same of the apostles. They withstood kingdoms and powers and stood firm until the very end, all by the Word.

The wise builder is in a deep love affair with the Word. Like the sons of Korah, and like the deer pants for the water, he craves the Word. He is a Word addict, and he's not interested in getting *sober* from this addiction. He meditates on the love letter of his Creator to him day in, day out—even in his sleep, he dreams about the Word. He digs into it for his own survival and growth, not to impress or intimidate others with his knowledge.

> *He builds his life on his truth and not on the Truth. He fails to understand that everything besides Christ is sinking sand.*

David was such a man; he was deeply in love with the Word of God. Let's take a moment to soak in his beautiful ode to the Word:

> The law of the LORD is perfect, converting the soul; The testimony of the LORD is sure, making wise the simple; The statutes of the LORD are right, rejoicing the heart; The commandment of the LORD is pure, enlightening the eyes; The fear of the LORD is clean, enduring forever; The judgments of the LORD are true and righteous altogether. More to be desired are they than gold, Yea, than much fine gold; Sweeter also than honey and the honeycomb. Moreover by them Your servant is warned, And in keeping them there is great reward. (Psa. 19:7–11)

BUILDING THE FAMILY ON THE ROCK

What a blessing it would be if we teach our children to build their house on Christ the solid rock from their childhood! Regarding the legacy of faith in Timothy's lineage, Paul said:

> I am reminded of your sincere faith, a faith that dwelt first in your grandmother Lois and your mother Eunice and now, I am sure, dwells in you as well. (2 Tim. 1:5 ESV)

Most children believe their parents are perfect. That may be God's way of giving parents a head start on molding their children before external agents come into play. It's easier to mold a child at 5 than at 15. Once this golden opportunity is gone, it may be difficult to get it back; however, we should not despair. With God all things are possible (Matt. 19:26). God has a track record of fixing seemingly hopeless situations. Your *lost* child can be restored by the grace of God.

Always pay close attention to the state of your child's soul. Education, entertainment, sports, talents, and physical health are great but are secondary to the state of their souls. We should be careful not to place our own economic empowerment over raising godly children. Hell is always searching the womb, both physically and spiritually. King Herod killed many babies and toddlers, all to get rid of baby Jesus. While some people may have selfish reasons not to have children, it's unfortunate to have children we cannot commit to raising in line with God's

> *The wise builder loves the truth, even if it makes him uncomfortable. He understands that the veracity of the truth is not dependent on the immediate comfort it affords.*

standard. If we value our children getting good academic grades over their spiritual growth, we may soon discover the danger of knowledge without God.

By nature, children would not choose the way of God. It's up to the parents to guide them towards and along the right path. Let us train our children in the way they *should* go, and not in the way they *would* go. We should help them find and value the solid foundation of Christ. It begins with us; we can't give what we don't have.

BUILDING THE SOCIETY ON THE ROCK

We often ask, "What is wrong with the world?" Crimes, moral decadence, wars, pestilences, violent riots, racism, and corruption are some challenges with which our world is grappling. Is it because we have neglected God? It seems societies originally built on godly principles are trying hard to eradicate Him from their consciousness.

Intelligent citizens without the moral rectitude to guide the use of their intelligence are often ruthless in politics, family, and business. An African proverb says, "A river that forgets its source will surely run dry." As a society, we are deliberately striking at and destroying our foundation as if to see what the end point of such an experiment would be—and we may soon find out.

No society announces it wants to destroy its own foundation. Destruction of a godly foundation is often disguised as freedom and empowerment. Promiscuity is no longer the dearth or death of moral purity; it's the freedom to choose and live freely. Drunkenness is simply a fun-filled rite of passage to adulthood. Abortion is no longer the death of a baby, but the freedom and right to choose. Divorce is no longer the death of a family; it's time to explore options and find our happiness. Impudence is nothing more than assertiveness. Unlimited borrowing is no longer a dearth of financial responsibility but freedom to get instant gratification.

> *Most children believe their parents are perfect. That may be God's way of giving parents a head start on molding their children before external agents come into play.*

Who doesn't like freedom and empowerment? Thus, we are encouraged to gulp down these poisons with sweetening additives and carefully worded labels. As if re-labelling *poison* as *not too tasty* makes it less deadly. To Eve, disobeying God was not death; it was instead a pathway to becoming as free and powerful as God. A proverb loosely translated says, "Banana rot is often mistaken for ripening." What we call freedom, God calls the sure path that leads to death and destruction.

Our children are our future as a society. Hence, the constant attempt by some governments and interested groups to indoctrinate them from childhood. Some governments appear intent on taking over parenting from parents. If the devil can't get us, he always tries to get us to leave something or someone behind. Pharaoh asked Moses and Aaron, "Go, serve the LORD your God, but who are they that shall go?" (Exo. 10:8 KJV). Moses answered him, saying,

> We will go with our young and our old, with our sons and with our daughters, with our flocks and with our herds will we go; for we must hold a feast unto the LORD. (Exo. 10:9 KJV)

He further said, "Our livestock also shall go with us; not a hoof shall be left behind" (Exo. 10:26 NLT). We should also boldly tell the devil that we will worship the Lord with our young, old, sons, daughters, and all. *Not a hoof will be left behind!*

BUILDING THE LOCAL CHURCH ON THE ROCK

The church—the body of Christ—is uniquely equipped to help in fixing damaged foundations of families and societies. But the church must get its own foundation right first. Have we placed charisma, fame, money, talents, or numerical growth above our spiritual foundation? A revival is not just about seeing the unsaved get saved; it also involves awakening the lukewarm saints. In fact, the revival must start with the saints before it can spread to the world. To transform the world, we must first be transformed by the Word.

Let us spend more time seeking the Lord in worship, Bible study, prayer, fasting, and evangelism than we do on special effects and entertainment. We must pay special attention to building the next generation. Do we expose tender souls to spiritual leaders that we would never allow near our own biological children? Do we ensure that the quality of our spiritual leaders is not compromised? Are the church workers diligent, intentional, and intense as beaten oil for the lamps of the sanctuary? (Exo. 27:20). Ministers must preach Christ only for Christ's sake—not for fame, money, ambition, influence, power, rivalry, or pride.

> *No society announces it wants to destroy its own foundation. Destruction of godly foundation is often disguised as freedom and empowerment.*

Some of the foundational Biblical truths which the church should not compromise on are:

1. Inerrancy of the Bible (Deut. 4:2; Mt. 5:18; 2 Pet. 1:20–21; Rev. 22:19).
2. Oneness of God (Deut. 6:4; Mark 12:29).
3. Universal sinful nature of humanity (Gen. 6:5; Isa. 53:6; Rom. 3:23).
4. Deity of Christ (John 8:58; Col. 2:9, Heb. 1:1–5; Rev. 22:13).
5. Virgin birth of Christ (Isa. 7:14; Luke 1:34–35; 1 John 4:9).
6. Substitutionary death of Christ (Isa. 53:5; Gal. 3:13; Heb. 2:9).
7. Bodily resurrection of Christ (Psa. 16:10; John 21:26–27; Acts 2:23–24).

8. Salvation by faith in Christ alone (John 6:28–29; Rom. 5:1; Gal. 3:24).
9. The imminent Second Coming of Christ (Matt. 26:64; Acts 1:11; Rev. 3:11).
10. Resurrection of the dead for judgment according to their deeds (Dan. 12:2; John 5:28–29; Rev. 20:13).

HOPE FOR FAULTY FOUNDATIONS

The parable of the wise and foolish builders teaches us it is better to get our foundation right at the very start. Unfortunately, that doesn't always happen. "If the foundations are destroyed, what can the righteous do?" (Psa. 11:3). The righteous can humbly go back to God in prayer.

We should seek God's guidance, both directly and through wise counsel, as we prayerfully examine our foundation for any flaws or vulnerabilities. It's time for us to return to our Father, the Architect. Let's stay active and positive, not succumbing to inactivity or despondency. Let's go back to God. For "after two days will He revive us: in the third day He will raise us up, and we shall live in His sight" (Hos. 6:2 KJV).

How much will repairs cost? That depends on the nature of the fault, the causes, the extent, and the effects. Don't go for a shoddy fix. It will only make a bad situation worse. The question is: Are you ready for a change? Are you willing to pay the price? Are you willing to have your damaged foundation ripped out from under you? Are you prepared to be pushed out of your comfort zone and be confronted with inconvenient truths? Are you willing to have your lifelong philosophies torpedoed, arguments left at the foot of the Cross, and your *truth* subjected to the Truth? If your answer is yes, congratulations! God is still in the business of fixing broken foundations. His promise to us is that "the glory of this latter house shall be greater than of the former" (Hag. 2:9 KJV). Amen.

> *In fact, the revival must start with the saints before it can spread to the world. To transform the world, we must first be transformed by the Word.*

Chapter 3

THE MUSTARD SEED

Here is another illustration Jesus used: "The Kingdom of Heaven is like a mustard seed planted in a field. It is the smallest of all seeds, but it becomes the largest of garden plants; it grows into a tree, and birds come and make nests in its branches."

MATTHEW 13:31–32 (NLT)

This parable is one of the seven (or eight, if you count the Household Treasures account in v. 52) parables Jesus told in Matthew chapter 13 to describe the kingdom of God. It's recorded in all three synoptic Gospels (Matt. 13:31–32; Mark 4:30–32; Luke 13:18–19). However, the Matthean account provides us with the most supporting information, as it includes one parable before and another after the current parable, all three parables addressing the same subject.

Of the three collocated parables, the parable of the mustard seed and the parable of the yeast have the most in common. Their emphasis is on how the kingdom of God has small beginnings but keeps growing until its influence becomes significant and ubiquitous. Like the shoot God planted on the lofty mountain discussed in Ezekiel 17:22, the kingdom of God is planted by God Himself. The small shoot would produce branches, bear fruit, and become a majestic cedar (Ezek. 17:23).

FROM SEED TO SHRUB

Imagine being tasked with finding a mustard seed randomly dropped on a farm. It may be extremely difficult to locate the seed amid the weeds and other plants on the farm—assuming a bird or rodent hasn't eaten it already. It's that small. In contrast, if you were asked to locate a mustard shrub, that would be a pretty simple task. This applies to most seed-tree pairs, and that's the crux of this parable: Big things often have small beginnings.

Many are hung up on whether the mustard seed is indeed the smallest of all seeds or whether its plant is the largest of all trees. Jesus' intent was not to give His hearers a lecture on botany. Rather, His intention was to capture their imaginations and take them on a journey that would make the message more accessible and leave a lasting impression on them. He was speaking to a local lay audience, not at an international conference of botanists.

As observed in most cultures, literary devices are often used to emphasize messages. For example, when a speaker says, "I've been here all day," the audience understands she doesn't literally mean she has been at the reference location since 12 a.m. Or our common use of *sunset*, even though we know the sun never actually sets. These are literary devices that make everyday conversations relatable. The former is a hyperbole used to emphasize that the speaker has spent a long time at the location.

In most cultures, there's a simile or metaphor for how tiny an object can be—not a scientific fact per se, but a common and relatable linguistic usage in the culture. According to the theologian Alfred Plummer, the Jews of Jesus' day would say, "as small as a mustard seed" when emphasizing how small an object was.[1] Additionally, there's an allusion to the smallness of a mustard seed in the Mishnah (the first major written collection of Jewish oral traditions): "And if there was a standing water, even like [as small as] a mustard seed, it joins" (M. Tahorot 8:8).[2]

Jesus used the mustard seed a few more times in His teachings (Matt. 17:20; Luke 17:5–6). Well, He could have said "as small as a quark," and then proceed to lecture His audience about the Planck length. But of what benefit would that be to them? It was more instructive to use the mustard seed, which a local farmer understood as the smallest seed he could plant on his farm, than use some esoteric examples.

It's not clear whether the mustard seed Jesus spoke about is the black mustard (*Sinapis nigra or Brassica nigra*) or the common (white) mustard (*Sinapis alba or Brassica hirta*). Black mustard seeds are only about a millimeter in diameter, but the plants can grow up to 1–4 m high. If the conditions are right, a mustard plant can grow large enough to provide nests for birds. The idea conveyed in the parable is that a tiny mustard seed, under the right conditions, will grow into a big plant in due time.

NOT TOO SMALL TO MAKE IMPACT

The parable applies primarily to the humble beginnings of the kingdom of God. It started small but see what it has grown into! The faith that began in an obscure part of Judea is now shared by billions of people worldwide.

God often sends us great trees hidden in tiny seeds, and if we are not careful, we may be discouraged by such small beginnings. He does this to stretch our limits and strengthen our faith. Joseph might have been satisfied with being a successful shepherd, but God had much bigger plans for him. He wanted him to become the prime minister of probably the greatest nation on earth at the time. What were the chances that a little shepherd boy, a foreigner no less, would one day become the prime minister of Egypt? An Egyptian nobleman's son would have been a better and surer candidate for such a dream.

> But God chose the foolish things of the world to shame the wise; God chose the weak things of the world to shame the strong. God chose the lowly things of this world and the despised things—and the things that are not—to nullify the things that are. (1 Cor. 1:27–28 NIV)

That is how God works. He does that "so that no one may boast before Him" (1 Cor. 1:29 NIV). He said, "I am the LORD; that is My name! I will not give My glory to anyone else, nor share My praise with carved idols" (Isa. 42:8 NLT).

The visions God gives us are such that we can't realize them using our own strength. Hence, when they become a reality, we can clearly see that it wasn't because of our acumen or prowess. It could only have been God. Our success may appear so improbable, or even impossible, that it attracts people who are awestruck and can only exclaim, "This must be God!"

We shouldn't be discouraged by the apparent impossibility of fulfilling our God-inspired dreams. A few loaves and fish can feed a multitude when breathed upon by God. Some excuses people often come up with to discount themselves are: "I'm too young," "I'm just one person," or "I'm just a woman." Other infamous entries include, "I make no difference," "I have no platform or influence," or "I have no talent." These people belittle themselves, forgetting that with God on their side, victory is assured.

We may belittle ourselves and believe we are of little worth. We may even believe that underestimating ourselves is a sign of humility. No, it's not. Belittling oneself is an affront to the omnipotence of God. Do we really know what God can accomplish through us? He brought the entire universe into existence just by His Word! Sometimes, we think and act as if we have doubts about God's ability to handle our *complicated* situations.

> *God often sends us great trees hidden in tiny seeds, and if we are not careful, we may be discouraged by such small beginnings.*

They may look complicated to us, but not to Him. How big are your challenges compared to the universe or the billions of lives—humans, animals, and plants—that God sustains every single day?

Gideon saw himself as insignificant. He was so scared of the marauding Midianites that he was hiding and threshing his grain in a winepress. Yet God ironically called him "You mighty man of valour!" He must have looked around to see if the angel was addressing someone else. "Definitely not me, a coward threshing grain in the winepress." The world, and even Gideon, could only see a coward, yet God only saw a mighty man of valour—a mustard tree hiding inside the mustard seed.

What made Gideon a mighty man of valour was not confidence, which he obviously lacked—nor wisdom. He was a mighty man of valour because the Lord was with him (Jugd. 6:12). Imagine the joy and empowerment that come with being addressed by none other than the God of the entire universe as a mighty man of valour. While we often see obvious failures in people and situations, God sees hidden successes in them. Stop undermining yourself. Humility is seeing yourself as God sees you—no more, no less.

IT KEEPS SPREADING

Another important point about a mustard plant is that many farmers considered it an annoying weed, as it would spread easily and extensively until it took over the entire farm. The Mishnah places restrictions on the planting of mustard seeds for the same reason:

> But if there were three patches, he shalt not sow them with mustard, for then the field as a whole looks like a field of mustard. (M. Kilayim 2:9)[3]

Having mustard plants proliferating in a field would have made it impossible to fulfill the commandment against mixing two kinds of seed in the same field (Lev. 19:19; Deut. 22:9). The mustard plants were deemed to *defile* or *corrupt* other crops. Similarly, many people, including powerful rulers, saw—and still see—Christianity as an annoying invading force that throws everything into chaos. It was, and still is, considered vulgar and incompatible with the grandiose visions of most political leaders.

Empires needed their soldiers to be warlike and hardened. In contrast, Christianity espouses virtues such as humility, kindness, and forgiveness. This would have easily threatened many empires with the fear that the spread of Christian ethics would undermine their often-brutal desire to conquer kingdoms. Regardless, the gospel spreads rapidly in the hostile garden of the world, just like the mustard seed.

> *We may even believe that underestimating ourselves is a sign of humility. No, it's not. Belittling oneself is an affront to the omnipotence of God.*

What is that *small* idea God has placed in your heart? Are you waiting for Him to increase it before you step out in faith? Run with the vision. It will grow. God can do so much with *so little*. As you step out in faith, the vision grows, and your faith is strengthened as well. The faith that's not growing is a dying one. Ours is the ever-increasing, blossoming faith. Your heart, not your situation, is the fertile ground in which your faith grows. That's why it can grow regardless of the situation or opposition you face. In that tiny seed lies a forest of trees.

Has God laid it in your heart to support a ministry, but you are ashamed of the tiny resources you have? Give whatever you have and watch as God multiplies it. Be encouraged by the story of the mustard seed of the Christian faith that started with a handful of disciples but has turned into a universal church with billions of believers thriving in the world today.

THE BIRDS

"And birds come and make nests in its branches" (Matt. 13:32 NLT). Some believe the birds in the parable symbolize evil agents sent to destroy the mustard tree (like the bird that ate the seeds in the parable of the sower). This interpretation assumes that once a character is used in a particular sense in a part of the Scripture, it can't be used in any other sense elsewhere. Parables, by nature, are not subject to such rigid constraints. It's more accurate to interpret the role of each character in a parable by considering the intent and context of the parable.

There's no indication whatsoever to show that the birds in this parable came to attack the mustard tree. Rather, the text clearly shows they came to make their nests in its branches. To Jesus' original audience, the imagery of birds fluttering around happily and nesting in a mustard tree would have been a familiar theme. The birds represent people—from all nations, tribes, and tongues—who will find solace in the kingdom of God. Apostle John described this glorious assembly in the book of Revelation:

> After these things I looked, and behold, a great multitude which no one could number, of all nations, tribes, peoples, and tongues, standing before the throne and before the Lamb, clothed with white robes, with palm branches in their hands. (Rev. 7:9)

In God's kingdom, there's no discrimination along nationality, gender, social status, or racial lines.

For Christ Himself has brought peace to us. He united Jews and Gentiles into one person when, in His own body on the

Cross, He broke down the wall of hostility that separated us. (Eph. 2:14 NLT)

The kingdom is a nest for weary birds to rest, recharge, and nurture their young. A popular song penned by Clare Herbert Woolston (1856–1927) goes thus:

Jesus loves the little children, all the children of the world.
Red and yellow, black and white, all are precious in His sight.
Jesus loves the little children of the world.[4]

Whatever colour we are, we all belong to this kingdom and can find solace in it. Even tax collectors and harlots who received the saving grace of Christ found solace in the kingdom. "Jesus said to them, 'Assuredly, I say to you that tax collectors and harlots enter the kingdom of God before you'" (Matt. 21:31). Let's be wary of turning our local assemblies into tribal dens where only people who look like us are welcome.

STILL ON THE BIRDS

The same birds that made their nests in the branches of the mustard tree could have easily swallowed it when it was just a seed. The people who mock your God-given vision in its infancy may soon come to find solace in it, if you don't give up. Many believers are waiting for people to approve of and support their visions before they make a move. It's likely people will *swallow* the vision with unbelief, doubt, envy, or disdain. It's only if you follow through with your vision that the same people may come to nest in the blessings that it will become.

> *What is that small idea God has placed in your heart? Are you waiting for Him to increase it before you step out in faith? Run with the vision. It will grow. God can do so much with so little.*

The sinners who mock your faith today may come to you for help tomorrow when life bites hard into them. What if you allow their mockery to swallow your faith now? What would they rely on tomorrow?

The same Joseph whose dreams were disparaged by his brothers became their lifeline when famine struck the land. Don't be angry with the angry birds; just protect your mustard seed from them. A time will come, and soon may it be, when they can no longer be a threat to your vision. Rather, they would nest in its success—and maybe they would be happy then. "When a man's ways please the LORD, He makes even his enemies to be at peace with him" (Prov. 16:7).

HIDDEN AT FIRST, BUT NOT FOR TOO LONG

Another lesson from this parable is the silent nature of the inner workings of the Holy Spirit in the heart of a believer. He doesn't make noise. He works as silent as light, as unimposing as a mustard seed. Yet when His work is mature in the believer's life, it becomes so visible and bright that none can miss it. The believer becomes like the city on a hill that cannot be hidden (Matt. 5:14). This is God's modus operandi.

Spirit-filled believers do not need to go around screaming that they are filled with the Spirit. Wisdom is justified by all her children (Luke 7:35). Let the facts speak for themselves. Let our light so shine that all men can see and glorify God. Even miles away, one can see the silent light, whereas the loud noise has already attenuated.

> *The same Joseph, whose dreams were disparaged by his brothers, became their lifeline when famine struck the land.*

Jesus' disciples once asked Him to increase their faith (Luke 17:5). Rather than grant their request immediately, He encouraged them to be persistent with the faith they already had:

> He replied, "If you have faith as small as a mustard seed, you can say to this mulberry tree, 'be uprooted and planted in the sea,' and it will obey you." (Luke 17:6)

Faith works. It also grows, but its growth requires time. There are no shortcuts on the journey of faith. We must water and nurture our faith to maturity. Jesus started His ministry with twelve disciples, but on the Day of Pentecost, there were 120 disciples in the Upper room. The growth didn't stop there:

> Every day they continued to meet in the temple courts. They broke bread in their homes and ate together with glad and sincere hearts, praising God and enjoying the favour of all the

people. And the Lord added to their number daily those who were being saved. (Acts 2:46–47 NIV)

Rodney Stark,[5] the late professor of sociology and comparative religion at the University of Washington, estimated the growth of Christianity during its formative years. In his book *The Rise of Christianity*, he estimated that by 150 AD, just about 120 years after the resurrection of Jesus, the worldwide Christian population was around 40,000. A hundred years later (250 AD), the estimated number of Christians was 1.17 million! Even if these are just ballpark figures, this is still no mean feat, especially when one considers that Christians were intensely persecuted and brutally martyred during these periods.

Persistence is the key to growing our faith. Rather than seek a dramatic increase in faith, work diligently with the one you already have. Faith—even one as little as a mustard seed—can move mountains.

Chapter 4

THE WEDDING BANQUET

❦❦❦❦❦❦❦❦❦❦

Jesus also told them other parables. He said, "The Kingdom of Heaven can be illustrated by the story of a king who prepared a great wedding feast for his son. When the banquet was ready, he sent his servants to notify those who were invited. But they all refused to come! So, he sent other servants to tell them, 'The feast has been prepared. The bulls and fattened cattle have been killed, and everything is ready. Come to the banquet!' But the guests he had invited ignored them and went their own way, one to his farm, another to his business. Others seized his messengers and insulted them and killed them. The king was furious, and he sent out his army to destroy the murderers and burn their town. And he said to his servants, 'The wedding feast is ready, and the guests I invited aren't worthy of the honor. Now go out to the street corners and invite everyone you see.' So, the servants brought in everyone they could find, good and bad alike, and the banquet hall was filled with guests. But when the king came in to meet the guests, he noticed a man who wasn't wearing the proper clothes for a wedding. 'Friend,' he asked, 'how is it that you are here without wedding clothes?' But the man had no reply. Then the king said to his aides, 'Bind his hands and feet and throw him into the outer darkness, where there will be weeping and gnashing of teeth.' For many are called, but few are chosen."

MATTHEW 22:1–14 (NLT)

Thu parable of the wedding banquet shares some similarities with the parable of the great banquet found in Luke 14:16–24. However, there are significant differences between the two, and these warrant separate discussions for both. This parable has more plot twists than the parable of the great banquet. A king had prepared a wedding banquet for his son. When everything was ready, he sent his servants to inform his guests that they should join him, but all of them refused to come.

The king then sent a second group of servants to the guests, furnishing them with the details of the delicacies he had prepared for them. Still, the guests ignored the servants and went about their business. Some even became so angry that they insulted and killed some of the king's servants.

The third and final time around, the king did not send his servants. He sent his army to destroy the murderers and burn down their town. Afterwards, he sent his servants to go bring in anyone they could find, good or bad, to the wedding venue—and they filled the venue with this new set of guests. Upon seeing his guests, the king noticed one individual who was not appropriately attired for the occasion.

It is implied that the king had expected all his guests to either come dressed in a certain way or avail themselves of the provision he had made for their attire. He asked the offender why he was not properly dressed but received no answer, at which time his aides bound the offender and threw him out of the venue into the outer darkness.

ELABORATE TRADITIONAL WEDDINGS

In the Jewish culture of Jesus' day, the parents of the betrothed would arrange the marriage contract, and the bride and groom would not meet officially until it was signed. After the signing of the contract, the people considered the couple married but still expected them to live apart until the time of the marriage ceremony. The bride remained with her parents, while the groom would leave to prepare for their future home. When the groom had set up their home, he would return for his bride. The marriage ceremony would then take place, and the wedding banquet would follow. The weddings were usually elaborate and could last for up to a week.

Such elaborate weddings are not unique to the Jews. Many cultures spread around the world have similarly extensive marriage processes. For example, the Yoruba tribe of West Africa has an elaborate and demanding marriage process, which in the past consisted of eight steps more or less, depending on the subculture. These steps were not just ceremonial; they were designed to test the endurance of the couple, especially the groom.

The first step is the *search*, where the potential groom visits locations that provide him with a high chance of running into a future bride; for example, local streams, night markets, or events with many damsels in attendance.

The second stage is *notification*. Once the man finds a suitable spouse (many families preferred endogamous relationships), he informs his father, who then informs the oldest male (the patriarch) in their extended family. The patriarch appoints one of the respectable wives already married into their family to act as a go-between for the groom and the spouse.

The third step is a *background check*. The female go-between finds out all she can about the damsel to ensure she will be an excellent addition to the family. Her main quest is to discover whether the damsel is from a good and reputable family. Both families perform painstaking checks to uncover any family history of stubbornness, murder, divorce, indebtedness, laziness, insanity, leprosy, barrenness, impotence, etc. Additionally, many subcultures forbid consanguineous marriages (cousin marriages). Thus, the go-between has the added task of ensuring that the couple are not related by blood in both their patrilinear and matrilinear lineages.

The fourth stage is *divination*. The parents of the potential couple consult their deities to know if the union will be blessed. If the outcome is favourable, the relationship can become public knowledge at this point.

The fifth stage is *acceptance of proposal*. At this juncture, there are no more hide-and-seek games and meetings in obscure places. In some subcultures, the groom makes seven formal visits to the damsel. He does all the talking as he proposes to her on six of such visits, while she remains mute. She's not expected to speak to him until he pays to *unveil* or *release* her voice. On the seventh and final visit, he pays a specified amount to release her voice, and she finally speaks to him and accepts his proposal—or not.

The sixth stage is *family solicitation.* This is the stage where the man officially asks for the damsel's hand in marriage. Unlike the previous stage, which was largely between the couple, the elders of the families are involved in this stage. The patriarch of the damsel's extended family oversees this stage. He accepts the marriage proposal made by the patriarch representing the groom's family, and a date is set for the betrothal.

The seventh stage is the *betrothal* or *creation of the affinal bond.* It's usually the first public (outside of the two extended families) ceremonial request for the hand of the damsel in marriage. Finally, the couple are getting formally engaged. Symbolic engagement items presented by the groom's family for prayers and invocations typically include kola nut (for fertility), honey (for sweetness), palm oil (for amelioration), bitter kola (for long life), alligator pepper (for unity and fertility), and salt (for preservation).

The eighth and final stage is the *wedding* or *transfer of the woman to the groom's lineage.* This is an elaborate ceremony during which the bride is handed over to the patriarch of the groom's family, who will ensure that she is cared for and nurtured. Her family and friends follow her up to the doorstep of her new home. They pray for her and wash her feet with water to cleanse her of any bad luck. She steps on a calabash just before stepping into the house. It was believed in some quarters that the number of shards of the broken calabash portends the number of children she will have in the marriage.

She is forbidden to meet her groom in their new home at this time, as it is considered to bring bad luck. So, the groom stays away from their home as his bride approaches. Of course, he eventually finds his way back in to consummate the union. The bride's family proudly displays a piece of white cloth stained by the bride's virginal blood after her first sex act. This announces to the community that their daughter was married a virgin, and that they have done a great job in raising a decent woman.

CHRIST'S ROYAL WEDDING

If the weddings of commoners can be as elaborate as discussed above, imagine the pomp and pageantry that would accompany a royal wedding. Such was the case of the king in this parable. He had organized an elaborate wedding for his son, with no expenses spared. It cost him a lot but cost the guests nothing. All they had to do was simply accept and honour the invitation of their king. Such is the case of God and humanity. He has created a path of salvation for us. It cost Him everything, even His most precious treasure—His only begotten Son. He asks for nothing in exchange. Hear His invitation to us all:

> Ho! Everyone who thirsts, come to the waters; and you who have no money, come, buy and eat. Yes, come, buy wine and milk without money and without price. (Isa. 55:1)

Just as the guests contributed nothing to the wedding banquet, we contribute nothing to the gift of salvation, save our unconditional acceptance of it. Jesus paid it all! It's all of grace. "For by grace you have been saved through faith, and that not of yourselves; it is the gift of God, not of works, lest anyone should boast" (Eph. 2:8–9). All we have to do is to accept God's offer of salvation by faith. Grace gives it all; faith takes it whole.

The king could have sent his soldiers to enforce compliance, to drag the invited guests to the venue, or at least threaten them. But he gave them the choice to either honour him or not. He sent harmless servants to them to see what was truly in their hearts, beyond their lip service and eye-service. After all, they all must have sworn an allegiance to their king. But he wanted honour by choice, not by force. He wanted enthusiastic guests, not cowering slaves, at his table.

After their initial refusal, to remove any doubts, the king furnished them with details of all he had prepared for them, hoping that would convince them to show up. The menu included bulls, fattened cattle, the best of wines, and other delicacies. There's no hunger in the human soul that the heavenly buffet of grace cannot satisfy. There's no sin stain so deep that the blood of Jesus cannot wash away. "But where sin increased, grace increased all the more" (Rom. 5:20 NIV). The greater the sin, the greater the grace to deal with it. "For from His fullness we have all received, grace upon grace" (John 1:16 ESV).

God gave the Law through Moses as an introduction of His grace and mercy to the Israelites. It was meant to teach them how to live to please God and maintain order among themselves. But with Jesus came the fullness of grace. It is indeed *grace upon grace* for believers in Jesus Christ. Salvation, victory over sin, deliverance, divine healing, prosperity, and power to cast out demons and trample on serpents are some menus on the divine buffet.

The preacher of the gospel should take the time to clearly explain the *grace upon grace* of the gospel to his hearers. This way, he would fulfill his role as a witness (Matt. 24:14), and his hearers would not be able to attribute their rejection of the gospel to ignorance.

We shouldn't be deceived into thinking that ignorance is the main reason people reject the gospel. For the invited guests, ignorance was not an excuse; they got the menu on offer yet declined. For us as well, ignorance won't be an excuse. Stubbornness and rebellion are often the main reasons for rejecting God's invitation to salvation. The guests ignored the king's servants and stubbornly went about their business. The rebellious ones insulted and even killed some of the servants.

FOUR RESPONSES TO THE KING'S INVITATION

Human response to the divine invitation of salvation falls into four broad categories, in an increasing order of culpability: acceptance, disregard, mocking or scoffing, and assault or killing of the messengers. No human is worthy of this invitation. Even those who accept the invitation do not deserve it. It's all of grace.

Those who choose to disregard it show no interest in considering matters of their eternal destiny. They are too busy with the ever-present mundane affairs of life to *waste* their precious time on the out-of-sight hereafter. The mockers and scoffers are committed to ridiculing and shaming the messengers of the gospel into silence. Apostle Peter warned us about the scoffers:

> Most importantly, I want to remind you that in the last days scoffers will come, mocking the truth and following their own desires. They will say, "What happened to the promise that Jesus is coming again? From before the times of our ancestors, everything has remained the same since the world was first created." (2 Pet. 3:3–4 NLT)

The last group is the most vicious. They don't have the patience of the scoffers in slowly wearing down the messengers. They want them silenced with alacrity—so they attack and kill them.

These four groups have co-existed since the dawn of time and are still here with us. Where do you belong? Membership in the groups is dynamic. Some who attacked and killed the messengers of the gospel ended up becoming its messengers themselves. An excellent example is Saul of Tarsus, who was an accomplice to the murder of the first Christian martyr (Stephen). He was later transformed into the famous Apostle Paul, who was eventually killed for the sake of the same gospel.

Conversely, some scoffers were once believers whose faith has been shipwrecked. Concerning such people, Paul said:

> Cling to your faith in Christ, and keep your conscience clear. For some people have deliberately violated their consciences; as a result, their faith has been shipwrecked. Hymenaeus and Alexander are two examples. I threw them out and handed them over to Satan so they might learn not to blaspheme God. (1 Tim. 1:19–20 NLT)

THE KING'S SERVANTS

In this parable, the servants represent the saints, not angels—as angels cannot be killed. The highlighted role of the servants was to go out to inform the invited guests the feast was ready. In discharging their duty, they experienced rejection, disdain, beatings, and death. All of God's saints experience rejection and disdain from time to time, but some have the *special honour* of being beaten and killed for the sake of the God they represent. "Yet for Your sake we are killed all day long; we are accounted as sheep for the slaughter" (Psa. 44:22).

The dead servants represent the dead saints, some of whom are mentioned in Table 2. An interesting thing about these servants is that the parable never reported them causing their king any grief. They were sent, and they simply went. Though their feet were beautiful as they brought good tidings and preached peace (Isa. 52:7; Rom. 10:15), they were met with rejection, shame, and death. They were as tenacious as their king. They never gave up, even after multiple rejections and assaults.

God's saints are like soldiers behind enemy lines—like sheep sent among wolves. When rejected and attacked, rather than give up, they

> gently instruct those who oppose the truth. Perhaps God will change those people's hearts, and they will learn the truth. Then they will come to their senses and escape from the devil's trap. (2 Tim. 2:25–26)

They serve at the pleasure of their King. The palace is their source, their resource, and their recourse. No matter how far out they go, they always return to the palace, to their King. And their King never forgets their labour of love. He keeps a record of all the servants He has sent out to His rebellious subjects—and their fate. For "precious in the sight of the LORD is the death of His saints" (Psa. 116:15). He will surely avenge their blood at the appointed time. Notice what Jesus said about His accurate reckoning of the deaths of His servants:

There's no hunger in the human soul that the heavenly buffet of grace cannot satisfy. There is no sin stain so deep that the blood of Jesus cannot wash away.

> Therefore, indeed, I send you prophets, wise men, and scribes: some of them you will kill and crucify, and some of them you will scourge in your synagogues and persecute from city to city, that on you may come all the righteous blood shed on the earth, from the blood of righteous Abel to the blood of Zechariah, son of Berechiah, whom you murdered between the temple and the altar. (Matt. 23:34–35)

Jesus placed the blood of all His murdered servants, including Abel who was murdered close to the dawn of time, on the hands of the people of His nation. But He wasn't just addressing the people of His day; rather, He was addressing the murderous spirit working behind the scenes to instigate people against His servants. At its root, it is a spiritual battle—a battle between the Holy Spirit who inspires the servants and the evil spirit instigating the rebellious subjects.

Table 2: Some of God's Servants Beaten and Killed by His Subjects

Servant	Mode of death	"Offence" committed
Abel	Beaten to death	His offering was accepted by God
Jeremiah	Stoned to death (by his people)	Spoke against the people's sins
Isaiah	Sawn in two on the order of King Manasseh	Spoke against the people's sins
Zechariah, son of Jehoiada	Stoned to death in the Temple court-yard	Denounced the sins of his cousin, King Jehoash of Judah
Micaiah	Killed by King Joram (son of King Ahab)	He rebuked King Joram for Ahab's impiety
Amos	Tortured severely by Amaziah, the priest of Bethel. Mortally wounded with a club by Amaziah's son	He prophesied against Amaziah
Stephen	Stoned to death	Preached the gospel
Ezekiel	Executed by the leader of the Israelites in exile	Spoke against the people's sins
Several prophets and priests	Killed by King Saul, Jezebel & many evil rulers	Spoke against the sins of the people and their kings
Several New Testament saints	Killed by Nero & other emperors	Nero blamed them for the Great Fire of Rome, etc.

Despite the continuous rebellion of His subjects, God keeps sending His servants to them. Why does He continue to sacrifice His obedient servants for His rebellious subjects? Why not just abandon them to their fate? Why does He spread out His hands all day long to a rebellious people who walk in the wrong path, following their own thoughts? (Isa. 65:2; Rom. 10:21). Love. Yes, love keeps the King going after His rebellious subjects. His purpose for sending and resending His servants to His subjects is to bring them back to Himself.

> The Lord is not slack concerning His promise, as some men count slackness; but is longsuffering to us-ward, not willing that any should perish, but that all should come to repentance. (2 Peter 3:9 KJV)

God is unbelievably patient with His rebellious subjects, even at the expense of His obedient servants. Lamenting over Jerusalem, Jesus said, "How often I wanted to gather your children together, as a hen gathers her chicks under her wings, but you were not willing!" (Mat. 23:37).

TRUTH HURTS

People hate the truth so much that they would do anything to stop it, including killing its messengers. Zechariah, son of Jehoiada, comes to mind. King Jehoash (or Joash) was so infuriated by Zechariah's message against his and the people's rebellion that he ordered the people to stone him to death immediately.

It's sobering to note that Zechariah's father, Jehoiada, had shown King Jehoash so much kindness during his lifetime, yet the king repaid his kindness by having his son stoned to death (2 Chron. 24:22). Such is the murderous spirit working in the children of disobedience. They would easily forget kindness and destroy anyone who hurts their feelings with the truth. Yet the servants' passion is to speak for their King, not to please His subjects.

Expecting kindness from a subject animated by a murderous spirit is nothing but unmitigated naivety. Jesus, addressing this murderous spirit acting in the shadows, said to His listeners, "You are of your father the devil, and the desires of your father you want to do. He was a murderer from the beginning" (John 8:44).

Zechariah's dying words were, "May the LORD see what they are doing and avenge my death!" (2 Chron. 24:22 NLT). The Babylonian Talmud (Git. 57b; Sanh. 96b)[1-2] contains a bizarre story about the shed blood of Zechariah. During the destruction of Jerusalem and its Temple in 586 BC, Nebuzaradan, the commander of Nebuchadnezzar's guard, encountered the blood of Zechariah who had been murdered 250 years earlier. According to the account, when Nebuzaradan entered the Temple mount, he saw Zechariah's blood still seething from the Temple floor!

He coerced the priests to reveal to him the source of this strange ominous phenomenon. They explained to him that the blood belonged to a priest and prophet who was killed for prophesying the destruction of Jerusalem. Nebuzaradan reportedly took extreme measures to appease the seething blood. He slew thousands of the people, starting with the Torah scholars. Yet Zechariah's blood would not stop seething. Out of frustration, he approached the blood and cried out, "Zechariah, Zechariah, I have already destroyed their finest. Do you want me to massacre them all?" Immediately, the blood stopped seething.

Nebuzaradan was reportedly so touched by this macabre encounter that he contemplated repentance. He reasoned that if it took all the killings to appease the blood of just one man, it would require a lot more to atone for his own soul after killing so many people. He deserted his army and dispatched a last will to his house and converted to Judaism.

While there's no account of this story in the Bible, the moral of the story remains that the blood of the righteous cries out for vengeance. Starting with Abel, the blood of every slain saint cries to God for vengeance. "But the LORD said, 'What have you done? Listen! Your brother's blood cries out to Me from the ground!'" (Gen. 4:10 NIV).

If only sinners would realize that they are being spared solely because the blood of Jesus speaks better and louder than the quest for vengeance by the blood of the slain saints! His blood is pleading for mercy on behalf of the rebellious subjects. Hear how the Bible puts it:

> You have come to Jesus, the One who mediates the new covenant between God and people, and to the sprinkled blood, which speaks of forgiveness instead of crying out for vengeance like the blood of Abel. (Heb. 12:24 NLT)

But this will not continue forever. God will avenge His saints one day.

TIME'S UP!

Ultimately, the king's patience ran out. He sent in his army—not his servants this time around—to punish the rebellious subjects. They killed the rebels and burned down their town.

The ungodly often perceive God's patience as a sign of weakness. They keep pushing their luck by disregarding His outstretched hands of mercy, just like their ancestors who mocked Noah's ark for many years until the floods came. The guests invited in both cases, by Noah and the king, weren't worthy of the honour. Paul and Barnabas responded with this truth when opposed by the Jewish leaders in Antioch (Pisidian):

> Then Paul and Barnabas grew bold and said, "It was necessary that the word of God should be spoken to you first; but since you reject it, and judge yourselves unworthy of everlasting life, behold, we turn to the Gentiles." (Acts 13:46)

Those who reject the King's invitation inadvertently judge themselves unworthy of eternal life. God simply confirms their choice—eternally. "Because you have forsaken the LORD, He also has forsaken you" (2 Chr. 24:20). The King will not keep sending His servants indefinitely. He will soon send in His army to punish the recalcitrant rebels.

THE INDEPENDENT GUEST: I LIKE IT MY WAY

It is implied in the parable that the king had made provisions for wedding garments for his guests. But when he came in to greet them, he noticed one of them was not wearing the provided garment.

The Bible tells us more about the garment the King has provided for His guests:

> Let us be glad and rejoice and give Him glory, for the marriage of the Lamb has come, and His wife has made herself ready. And to her it was granted to be arrayed in fine linen, clean and bright, for the fine linen is the righteous acts of the saints. (Rev. 19:7–8)

The royal apparel is fine linen, clean and bright. It's the righteous acts of the saints. What a privilege it is for a believer to be clothed in this royal apparel! Yet many believers assume what beautifies them is their wealth, health, talents, prosperity, or the other perks of their walk with God. Many Christian ministries are built around these perks, with charismatic preachers helping to keep their audiences focused on them to the detriment of the righteous acts.

It is important to note that the guest without the appropriate garment was not naked. He just had on an inappropriate garment. What was he thinking to be dressed like that? Did he not notice the attire of the other guests?

People rarely do things without some reason—some sort of justification for what they do. When confronted with their sins or shortcomings, they can repent, but they often rather become defensive and seek to justify their actions or inaction. The more adamant they become, the more they argue, and the more reasonable their argument begins to sound to them—no matter how unreasonable it felt at the start.

One can win an argument and still lose one's soul. Winning is not always winning. Winning now is not necessarily winning then. The odd guest probably convinced himself that his garment was good enough for the wedding banquet. Yet when confronted by the king, he had no reply (v. 12). No matter the arguments we win in our heads to justify our actions now, when standing face to face with God, we will be speechless. All that seems reasonable now may seem too unreasonable to be voiced then. No one can win an argument against the King. "But the LORD is in His holy temple. Let all the earth keep silence before Him" (Hab. 2:20).

> *Though their feet were beautiful as they brought good tidings and preached peace, they were met with rejection, shame, and death.*

Godly wealth, health, and prosperity are good, but nothing beautifies a believer like righteousness. We are called to worship the LORD in the beauty of holiness (1 Chron. 16:29; Psa. 29:2; 96:9; 110:3). We find several references in the Bible to clothing being used as an analogy for behaviours, either pleasing to God or displeasing to Him (Rom. 13:14; Eph. 4:22–24; 1 Pet. 5:5). The Bible admonishes us to put off our old self with its sinful deeds—comparing it to taking off a garment—and to put on the new self, beautified in holiness.

> You were taught, with regard to your former way of life, to put off your old self, which is being corrupted by its deceitful desires; to be made new in the attitude of your minds; and to put on the new self, created to be like God in true righteousness and holiness. (Eph. 4:22–24)

We shouldn't confuse the *righteous acts* with the works of the flesh trying to earn divine approval. It's the grace of God generating these righteous acts in us, as we work in partnership with Him to bring forth fruit worthy of repentance (Matt. 3:8).

PERISHED AT THE TABLE

The guest without the royal apparel was bound hand and foot and thrown into outer darkness, where there would be weeping and gnashing of teeth. Who would have thought that a man who honoured the invitation would end up with a fate akin to that of those who did not honour the invitation!

Some believers think it doesn't matter how they live their lives. They believe they are forever saved by accepting the invitation and sitting at the banquet table. Yet this parable clearly shows one can perish at or away from the table. One can start out right and still miss it. We need to start out right, continue strong, and not turn to the left or right (Josh. 1:7; Prov. 4:27), so that we can end well. "But he that shall endure unto the end, the same shall be saved" (Matt. 24:13 KJV).

> *No matter the arguments we win in our heads to justify our actions now, when standing face to face with God, we will be speechless.*

We cannot serve God lawlessly or just how we please. Freedom without boundaries is free doom. It was poetic justice that the first thing taken away from the disobedient guest was his freedom— the freedom he cherished so much, to the point of acting lawlessly at the banquet. He was bound hand and foot.

At the beginning, sin may feel like unfettered freedom to do as one pleases. Yet in the end, nothing is as enslaving as sin. It may start as fun, but it soon becomes an addiction as binding as a strong chain.

The guest was led away to outer darkness with his hands and feet bound in chain. He was led away from the king, his son, the bride, and the other guests.

Likewise, the negligent and obstinate believer will be led away from the presence of the King, His Son, and the bride (the fellowship of the saints). He will be led away from kingdom principles, provisions, joys, light, and delights—away into the outer darkness where there is grief, remorse, and misery.

> We cannot serve God lawlessly or just how we please. Freedom without boundaries is free doom.

In our quest for *authenticity* and independence, let's be wary of abandoning the pattern laid down by God. "Let him who thinks he stands take heed lest he fall" (1 Cor. 10:12), and let's "see to it that no one falls short of the grace of God" (Heb. 12:15 NIV). Since we know that "many are called, but few are chosen" (Matt. 22:14), let's be diligent to make our call and election sure so that we won't stumble (2 Pet. 1:10). So help us God!

Chapter 5

THE GREAT
BANQUET

Jesus replied with this story: "A man prepared a great feast and sent out many invitations. When the banquet was ready, he sent his servant to tell the guests, 'Come, the banquet is ready.' But they all began making excuses. One said, 'I have just bought a field and must inspect it. Please excuse me.' Another said, 'I have just bought five pairs of oxen, and I want to try them out. Please excuse me.' Another said, 'I just got married, so I can't come.' "The servant returned and told his master what they had said. His master was furious and said, 'Go quickly into the streets and alleys of the town and invite the poor, the crippled, the blind, and the lame.' After the servant had done this, he reported, 'There is still room for more.' So, his master said, 'Go out into the country lanes and behind the hedges and urge anyone you find to come, so that the house will be full. For none of those I first invited will get even the smallest taste of my banquet."

LUKE 14:16–24 (NLT)

This parable is similar to the parable of the wedding banquet narrated in Matthew 22:1–14 and discussed in the previous chapter. Jesus told this parable in response to the comment, "Blessed is the man who will eat at the feast in the kingdom of God!" uttered by a guest sitting at the dining table in the home of a prominent Pharisee who had invited Jesus to dinner. Hence, the great banquet referenced here is the feast in the kingdom of God.

In this parable, a man prepared a great feast and sent out many invitations to his (we can assume) acquaintances and friends. On the day of the feast, all of them came up with excuses to justify their absences. The man was furious when he heard their flimsy excuses. He ordered his servants to go quickly into the streets and alleys (probably the shady parts of town) to invite the poor, the crippled, the blind, and the lame—people not typically invited to banquets.

It appears some, or most, of the second set of invitees honoured the invitation. Yet there was still room for more at the banquet. The man sent his servants out for the third time, to go to the country lanes and behind the hedges to "urge anyone [they] find to come, so that the house will be full" (v. 23).

THE THREE CATEGORIES OF INVITEES

Note the changes in the targets, the urgency, and the tone of the invitations. The first target group was comprised of respectable people from the opulent parts of the town. People who had enough means to purchase land (landowners), several pairs of oxen, and could afford to take time off after their wedding. The tone of the message was simple and familiar, as if talking to longtime friends, "Come, the banquet is ready." Urgency was not particularly conveyed in the message, as the invitations assumed prior knowledge of the feast.

In terms of location, the second target group was a downgrade from the first. Though they were still located within the town, they lived in the squalid parts. Most cities have *dark* areas into which respectable people dare not enter. The second group came from such areas. The group comprised social misfits who were deemed *not presentable* at important occasions due to their physical and financial disabilities.

In addition, while the first group wouldn't need much assistance to find their way to the venue of the banquet, the second group would probably need financial or physical assistance to get there. For this group, the tone was less familiar and more urgent. This was an invitation to strangers who probably had no prior knowledge of the banquet or only heard about it through the grapevine.

The third and final group was not even within the city borders at all. They lived far away in the countryside (rural dwellers) and *behind* the hedges (likely foreigners or outcasts behind the border lines).

The second and third groups were the social outsiders. For the third group, the tone of the invitation had escalated to *urge*. The words *urgent* and *urge* share a common Latin ancestor *urgere*, which means to *press*, *entreat*, or *drive*. It indicates that the servants tried earnestly and persistently to persuade the third group to come to the banquet.

The tone of the invitations escalated from *familiar* to *formal*, and then to persistent *persuasion*. The parable closes with the host vowing that no one from the first group would get even the smallest taste of his banquet.

BETWEEN GOD AND ISRAEL

The master in the parable represents God, while the servants that went out with the invitations represent the prophets and preachers that God sent out to Israel and the nations. The first group represents the Jewish nation, who were the first recipients of God's invitation to the great banquet. Regarding this truth, Apostle Paul boldly declared:

> For I am not ashamed of this Good News about Christ. It is the power of God at work, saving everyone who believes— *the Jew first* and also the Gentile. (Rom. 1:16 NLT, emphasis mine)

Unfortunately, "He [Jesus] came to His own, and His own did not receive Him" (John 1:11).

The guest who made the statement that prompted Jesus to tell this parable was probably under the illusion that only the Jews would partake in the *exclusive* feast in the kingdom of God. This guest was probably one of those who were struggling to get seats of honour beside Jesus at the dining table (Luke 14:7). He must have felt special sitting that close to Jesus. Jesus told this parable to repudiate the notion that the kingdom of God is exclusive to the Jews.

The second group represents the Samaritans who though were affiliated with the Jews—as implied by their being located within the city but in the slummy parts—were deemed rejects and outcasts.

The third group represents the Gentiles and outsiders to the Jewish commonwealth. This distinction is obvious in the mandate Jesus gave His disciples before the Day of Pentecost.

But you shall receive power when the Holy Spirit has come upon you; and you shall be witnesses to Me in Jerusalem, and in all Judea and Samaria, and to the end of the earth. (Acts 1:8)

Judea was south of Jerusalem, while Samaria was to its north. Jesus instructed that the gospel, originating in Jerusalem, should be spread first to the Jews in Judea, then to the Samaritans in Samaria, and then to the ends of the earth.

Further, when Jesus sent out His disciples on their initial evangelical mission, He commanded them not to go to the Gentiles (the third group) or the Samaritans (the second group). Their focus was the Jewish nation (the first group). Matthew put it this way:

These twelve Jesus sent out and commanded them, saying: "Do not go into the way of the Gentiles, and do not enter a city of the Samaritans. But go rather to the lost sheep of the house of Israel." (Matt. 10:5–6)

The plan of God is that His Law and the gospel would be revealed first—but not only—to the Jews based on His covenant with their forefathers (Abraham, Isaac, and Jacob). God's intent was to project and display the Jewish nation as a model of what obedience to Him looks like. This model was meant to attract, in due course, the Samaritans and all the nations of the earth to the God of Israel.

However, the rejection of the gospel by the Jews accelerated the opening of the gospel to the Samaritans and the rest of the world. In all, God's promise to Abraham still stands: "In your seed [Jesus] all the nations of the earth shall be blessed, because you have obeyed My voice" (Gen. 22:18).

EXCUSES UNLIMITED

The first group came up with several excuses for missing the great banquet. One said he just bought a field and must inspect it. Another said he just bought five pairs of oxen and wanted to try them out. The last person said he just got married and couldn't make it to the banquet.

These excuses appeared to be legitimate human endeavours revolving around commerce, industry, and marriage. Yet they exposed the value these invitees placed on the banquet and the host. The host saw his banquet as a *great* banquet and felt it was a privilege to extend the invitation to his friends and acquaintances. However, it seems the invitees did not share his sentiment.

Theirs was a value system problem. Our priorities are based on our values. The first group valued inspecting their field, trying out their oxen, and staying indoors with a new wife above attending the great banquet. Of course, had they valued the banquet and the host, all these activities could have been done at other times. The field and the oxen could have been inspected before purchase or at some other time, and the new wife could have been taken along to the banquet.

It is sad but commonplace to see believers neglect their fellowship with God while tending to His blessings in their lives. It is possible for us to prioritize possessions, relationships, children, spouses, and even ministry above God in our lives. If that happens, the blessings may become a curse.

Their flimsy excuses revealed the true value they placed on the host and his banquet. The same thing applies to us today. Some of our excuses may be illegitimate, but even the legitimate ones are wrongly prioritized above God. Prayer and Bible study often become the last items to be ticked off our daily checklist, after we have attended to the *more important* issues.

Spouses given to us by God have drawn many away from fellowship with Him. For some, their last evangelical outreach was before they got married. They are legitimately busy with family life and would probably run back to God only when troubles arise. Unbridled success is an enemy of the soul.

There is no excuse good enough to reject God's invitation—none. Though you may think that business deal cannot wait, remember that some people who died today were probably on their way to very urgent business meetings. Yet after their death, the world moves on without them, and quickly too. The world's system uses people, hollows out their souls, and spits them out whenever it feels they have nothing more to offer.

Many are currently in positions previously occupied by people who were once considered indispensable. Except that they were quickly replaced as soon as they had outlived their usefulness to the organization.

Indeed, life goes on. Never leave your salvation until another time. Tomorrow may never come.

FREE WILL IS SACROSANCT

The banquet host did not force the unwilling invitees into attending his banquet, though he probably had the means to enforce compliance. We can learn from this that no matter how much we care for people, we cannot force them into God's kingdom or override their will. God respects free will so much that He doesn't override it, even when people use their free will against Him. Even if we mandate worship and drag people (including our children) to church, we cannot win over their hearts by force. The body may be with us, but the heart is not.

As the invitees had the free will to make their choices, the host also had the free will to make his. He banned them from his banquet forever. They made a choice to avoid his banquet; he made their choice permanent. The sinner here on earth makes the choice to stay away from God; God in eternity simply makes his choice permanent.

If only sinners understood the full implication of being cut off from God, they would not reject His invitation. Unfortunately, they do not realize that, even for an atheist, living on earth is not equal to being totally cut off from God. "For in Him we live and move and have our being" (Acts 17:28). We all owe our breath, motion, bodies, health, and everything to the benevolence of God.

> *God's intent was to project and display the Jewish nation as a model of what obedience to the Word of God looks like.*

Even sinners who reject God here on earth are still enjoying His benevolence. "For He makes His sun rise on the evil and on the good, and sends rain on the just and on the unjust" (Matt. 5:45). In essence, here on earth, the sinner gets to keep the gifts while rejecting the Giver. He believes *Mother Nature*, not God, has blessed him with all these gifts.

God's benevolence may warp his mind into thinking that rejecting the Giver is not such a bad idea after all. Unfortunately for him, the earth is not the real total separation from God; hell is. By the time he realizes this, it's probably too late. It is like a spoilt child claiming not to have anything to do with his estranged parents, while living in their house, using their cars, working in their company, and eating their food. When the parents finally cut him off from everything, he comes to realize how ungrateful and ignorant he has been all the while.

The rejection by the first group opened the door for the second and third groups. In fulfillment of Hosea 2:23, those whom God called "Not My people," He now tells, "You are My people." They, in turn and with gratitude, say to Him, "You are our God." The Gentiles can now call God *Abba, Father!*

We should be wary of the familiarity that breeds contempt. The closer we think we are to God, the more likely we are to treat Him lightly. That was the mistake the first group made. They got too familiar with the host to take his invitation seriously.

A colleague once told me he disliked Christianity because the concept of heaven seemed to him like an exclusive club of sanctimonious people. Yet we see from this parable that rather than have empty seats at the banquet, the host extended the invitation to all and sundry. He possibly delayed the start of the feast to have more people come in from the countryside and outside the hedge, even those who needed assistance to get to the banquet.

That doesn't sound like a deliberately discriminatory event. Heaven is not an exclusive club for some spiritual aristocrats. However, an invitation with directions to the banquet is required. Without it, we wouldn't know how to get there; for "no one knows the Son except the Father, and no one knows the Father except the Son and anyone to whom the Son chooses to reveal him" (Matt. 11:27).

> *There is no excuse good enough to reject God's invitation—none. Though you may think that business deal cannot wait, remember that some people who died today were probably on their way to very urgent business meetings.*

God's love is perfectly balanced by His holiness, and anyone who wishes to enter His kingdom must be holy. Hear what John said about this in the book of Revelation:

> But there shall by no means enter it anything that defiles, or causes an abomination or a lie, but only those who are written in the Lamb's Book of Life. (Rev. 21:27)

God's high standard of holiness is not a discriminatory policy to keep people out of heaven. In fact, He has made the provision for everyone to be as holy as befitting the occasion. As highlighted in the similar parable of the wedding banquet, He has made special robes available for the guests.

It is ultimately pride or willful ignorance that makes one reject the gifts of God—love and holiness, perfectly blended. Pride makes people disparage God's free gift of salvation, while willful ignorance makes people either avoid facing the reality of their eternal destiny or disregard the revealed truth concerning their current state and its eternal consequences.

DON'T MISS THE FEAST

God does not delight in a heaven devoid of humans. So, He brought heaven down to us. He gains nothing by keeping people out of heaven. After all, the feast is already prepared. Heaven has enough room for anyone and everyone who would be saved. The blood of Jesus has already provided forgiveness for the sins of everyone who has ever lived and will ever live, even the people in hell.

Whether we accept this forgiveness is another question altogether. It's like the case of people who RSVP'd to a wedding invitation but failed to show up. The food is already prepared and having fewer people at the occasion would only lead to wastage. Thus, it is people, not God, who keep themselves out of heaven.

> *If only sinners understood the full implication of being cut off from God, they would not reject His invitation.*

The host is more committed to filling the banquet hall than any of the guests can ever be. Similarly, no matter how burdened we are for the salvation of souls, we can only share in part of God's burden. We can trust that He is more committed to the salvation of souls than we are. Let this comfort and encourage you whenever you are worried about the salvation of your loved ones—children, parents, siblings, friends, or spouses.

As believers, we can share in the host's burden by reaching out to people on the street, the alleys, the countryside, and even outside the hedge. Are you a guest at the table already? Don't feast alone. Why not reach out to the others you left behind? Now that you have been saved, try to bring others as well. There is nobody so lost or so far out in sin that God cannot save.

It is sad to note that some have missed the point of this parable and have used it to push anti-Semitic agendas. The aim of the parable is to get us all to take God's invitation to salvation seriously. It is not to condemn the Jews. It's not about nationality; it is about humanity. We tend to take for granted those closest to us, even if they are celebrated everywhere else. Truly, "a prophet is honoured everywhere except in his own hometown and among his relatives and his own family" (Mark 6:4 NLT).

God's high standard of holiness is not a discriminatory policy to keep people out of heaven. In fact, He has made the provision for everyone to be as holy as befitting the occasion.

It is a universal flaw, not a uniquely Jewish one. If Jesus had been of any other nationality, chances are He would have still *come to His own and they would have received Him not*. So, the moral of the parable is that we should be careful not to take the grace of God for granted.

The responses of the three groups mirror the responses to the preaching of Apostle Paul.

> And when they heard of the resurrection of the dead, *some mocked*: and others said, *we will hear thee again* of this matter … howbeit *certain men clave unto him and believed*. (Acts 17:32–34 KJV, emphasis mine)

When we hear His voice, we can mock, postpone acceptance until a more convenient time, or cleave to Him and believe. Many are called but few are chosen (Matt. 22:14). Remember that God's invitation has an expiry date and rejecting Him now may be reckoned as eternal rejection. "Today, if you will hear His voice, do not harden your hearts as in the rebellion" (Heb. 3:15).

Chapter 6

THE SOWER

He told many stories in the form of parables, such as this one: "Listen! A farmer went out to plant some seeds. As he scattered them across his field, some seeds fell on a footpath, and the birds came and ate them. Other seeds fell on shallow soil with underlying rock. The seeds sprouted quickly because the soil was shallow. But the plants soon wilted under the hot sun, and since they didn't have deep roots, they died. Other seeds fell among thorns that grew up and choked out the tender plants. Still other seeds fell on fertile soil, and they produced a crop that was thirty, sixty, and even a hundred times as much as had been planted!"

MATTHEW 13:3–8 (NLT)

In this parable, Jesus used four different soil conditions to illustrate how humans respond to the Word of God. The soil symbolizes the human heart, while the seed symbolizes God's Word. It appears the soil condition goes from worst to best.

The first (and worst) soil was the footpath where birds had easy access to the seeds and ate them—the seeds stood no chance. The second soil was the shallow soil with underlying rock. In this case, the seeds had a chance to germinate, and indeed sprouted quickly. The third was the thorny soil. In it, the seeds grew and survived for a while, until thorns choked them. In the fourth soil, which was the best, the seeds grew to maturity.

SEEDS ALONG THE FOOTPATH

The seeds that fell along the footpath represent the fate of God's Word in the hearts of people who neither understand nor believe it. Before the Word could take root in their hearts, the evil one (the devil) came and snatched it away. Footpaths are hardly amenable to seed growth, as constant trampling by humans and animals compacts the soil so much that it becomes impervious to seeds. Hence, any seeds dropped on it stay on the surface, unprotected and easy for birds to feast upon.

Birds can easily pick up the Word when it's not hidden in the heart. "Your Word I have hidden in my heart, that I might not sin against You" (Psa. 119:11). Like a treasure, the Word should be carefully hidden in the human heart where the Holy Spirit can brood upon it just like He brooded upon the waters during creation (Gen. 1:2).

The first course of attack by the enemy is to ensure that the Word does not sink into the human heart. The modern human has been numbed by so many activities that there's hardly any internal quietness that allows the Word to settle in. Continuous entertainment, social media, parades, parties, camping, work, school, and festivals are some of the activities that inundate the modern human with distractions. These make it difficult, if not impossible, for the seed of the Word to be sown in the heart.

How many people can watch just five minutes of preaching on TV when there are myriads of entertainment alternatives? This is a generation that's being entertained on its way to hell. Indeed, the preliminary challenge is to get the sinner to be quiet enough to hear the Word and let it sink in. If possible, the preacher should try to get the sinner away from distractions so that there's an opportunity for the Word to be received into the heart. Perhaps conviction may occur.

> *The first course of attack by the enemy is to ensure that the Word does not sink into the human heart.*

Be it in our churches or outside, we should minimize distraction as much as possible, particularly during sermon. Care should be taken to ensure that children, and even adults, do not become so addicted to entertainment and activities that they despise quiet contemplation. It is during such quiet periods that the Word sinks into the human heart and may germinate.

SEEDS ON THE SHALLOW, ROCKY SOIL

The seeds that fell on the shallow, rocky soil represent the fate of God's Word in the hearts of people who receive the Word and allow it to germinate, but not grow to maturity. This soil is an improvement on the footpath soil, as the seed has a chance to sink into the soil. However, because of the proximity of the underlying rock to the surface, the seed has no space to grow its root downward, so it rapidly springs upward. This is the condition of those who receive the Word with so much joy but with little to no understanding. They mistake the flamboyant emotions that accompany their hearing of the Word for the grasping and understanding of the truth.

When we prioritize our emotions or how others perceive us over how God sees us, we run the risk of sprouting too hastily, only to wilt at the slightest sign of trouble or persecution. It is God's desire that we take root downward as we bear fruit upward. "And the remnant who have escaped of the house of Judah shall again take root downward and bear fruit upward" (Isa. 37:31).

> *This is a generation that's being entertained on its way to hell.*

The bigger our shoots, the greater the attacks we attract. Thus, it's dangerous to bear shoots upward without deepening our root system which serves as our anchor when we are under attack. We should be careful not to become so focused on externalities that we forget to pay attention to our root, our *inner man* (2 Cor. 4:16).

The root is rarely as visible as the shoot. Similarly, the spiritual exercises that deepen our root are often not visible to the public. Feelings may be flowery, but they don't last. Likewise, a life driven by feelings is unstable, as it lacks the root system of conviction. Activities such as leading worship services and teaching Sunday school may expose us to the spotlight. While nothing is wrong with that, without a correspondingly strong root system, we may soon wither away under the scrutiny afforded by the spotlight. If the (spot)light on you is brighter than the light in you, you may eventually falter.

We should avoid mistaking social contagion—even of the religious type—for a personal encounter with Christ. People who follow popular trends and fads may show a lot of fervency in the heat of the moment, but they grow lukewarm as soon as the fad fades and something new comes along.

For such people, bombastic religious sloganeering is commonplace. They are addicted to the thrills of new programs, concerts, conferences, and events. The Word cannot fully transform them as they are unable to sit in calm contemplation. Their constant pursuit is finding the next *spiritual high*. They only associate with Jesus when it's trendy and doesn't demand any sacrifices. As soon as a price tag is attached to their profession, they balk at the Cross and find the next fad.

SEEDS ON THE THORNY SOIL

The seeds that fell on the thorny soil represent the fate of God's Word in the hearts of people who receive the Word, allow it to grow, but let it get choked by thorns or cares of life. Such hearts are crowded with the cares and worries of life. The seed grows and survives for a while, until the thorns choke it.

The longevity of the seed in this soil appears to be more than for the first two soils. This heart receives the Word, hides it inside, nourishes it, takes root downward, and bears shoot upward. It appears to be set for success. Yet it fails eventually. The anxieties of life choke the plant.

The Christian race is a marathon, not a sprint. It's a narrow path that has deep gullies on both sides, thus making it possible to fall either to the extreme right or to the extreme left. It takes the grace of God and caution to stay on the narrow path with lifelong consistency.

> *Care should be taken to ensure that children, and even adults, do not become so addicted to entertainment and activities that they despise quiet contemplation.*

Many unbelievers today are backsliders who initially started out as fervent Christians but gradually allowed the cares of life to strip them of their faith. Preoccupation with issues of life, even legitimate ones such as finances and ambitions, may soon tilt the heart away from the Word and its relationship with Christ. That is why Jesus warned us against fretting over our needs, even the ones as legitimate as food and drink. "Do not worry about your life, what you will eat or what you will drink" (Matt. 6:25).

This heart fails to prioritize Christ above all else. If there's a rivalry between God and Mammon in this heart, Mammon wins. We should prayerfully check the condition of our heart daily to ensure that thorns are not taking over our lot. At first, the thorns may be tiny and seem benign, but thorns are known for rapid and uncontrolled growth. With time, the little Mammon pleading for just a tiny spot soon becomes strong and takes over. A thorn often asks for just a foothold but ends up taking over the entire lot. That's why the Scripture says, "And do not give the devil a foothold" (Eph. 4:27 NIV).

There are several examples of people overtaken by thorns in the Bible. Demas forsook Paul and the faith because of his love for the world (2 Tim. 4:10). The rich young ruler loved mammon so much that he wouldn't follow Christ (Mark 10:17–27). And there was the interesting case of the man who got the most important call of his life to follow Jesus but turned it down and asked for a moratorium of one year to bury his father (Matt. 8:21–22).

The value system of a believer should differ from that of the world. Desire for wealth, fame, and power should not be the overarching influence in the life of a believer. We should avoid decisions and lifestyle choices that can drag us into the pervasive rat race of life. For example, debt can serve as a thorn that keeps our heart preoccupied at the expense of our faith. Living within our means can put our mind at rest and affords us the opportunity to develop our faith.

Both the thorns and the seed are competing for the same nutrients in the soil. Likewise, faith and fear compete for the same resources in our heart. One grows at the expense of the other. When faith grows, fear withers—and vice versa. Whenever we receive troubling news threatening our inner peace, we should take captive such news, thought, or information and make it obedient to Christ (2 Cor. 10:5). To accomplish this, we seek what the Word says concerning the situation, subjecting it—its facts and lies—to the truth of God's Word.

If the (spot) light on you is brighter than the light in you, you may eventually falter.

We pray with the Word. We declare the Word and keep declaring it until fear flees from our soul. This will be an impossible task if we do not guard our heart with all diligence (Prov. 4:23). Faith comes from hearing the Word of God (Rom. 10:17), but fear comes from hearing the word of Satan. For this reason, we must be careful about the things we allow into our heart.

If we set our heart on things above and not on earthly things (Col. 3:2), our heart will not tumble along with the vicissitudes of life. The peace of God that passes all understanding will guard our heart. If our faith must take on wings and soar, we must feed it with the Word. *For God's Word is the wind beneath the wings of faith.*

SEEDS ON THE GOOD SOIL

The good soil represents the fate of God's Word in individuals who receive and nurture it to full fruition. It's the heart that is honest and good. It believes and holds steadfastly to what it has received. It doesn't just believe for a while and stop. It continues to believe until the Word bears fruit, yielding a hundredfold, sixtyfold, or thirtyfold harvest.

The good soil is not an accident of nature. It is intentionally tilled, even ploughed, to prepare for the seed. Weeding is performed routinely to protect the growing crops. The good soil is the heart that continues to work out its salvation with fear and trembling (Phil. 2:12). Sadly, many believers saunter into worship services with no expectations or preparation in the place of prayer and waiting. The same thing happened during the earthly ministry of Jesus. He was occasionally thronged by enormous crowds who just wanted to satisfy their curiosity. Few had any serious expectations.

> *Likewise, faith and fear compete for the same resources in our hearts. One will have to grow at the expense of the other. When faith grows, fear withers—and vice versa.*

Many came empty, went back empty, and probably told some tall tale about what they had just witnessed. Some, however, were too expectant and desperate to be denied. For instance, the woman with the issue of blood did not come for sightseeing (Mark 5:25–34). She came prepared and with the expectation of receiving her miracle.

Many people touched Jesus, but she touched Him i*ndeed.* Her faith and expectation set up a potential difference between her and Jesus such that as soon as she touched Him, currents of virtue flowed out of Him to her, even without His explicit permission (Mark 5:30). "The sacrifices of God are a broken spirit, a broken and a contrite heart, O God, thou wilt not despise" (Psa. 51:17 KJV). She came prepared—broken, contrite, and expectant—and she was neither despised nor denied. After all, Jesus said, "The one who comes to Me, I will by no means cast out" (John 6:37).

The good soil does not waste the Word and the grace of God bestowed upon it (2 Cor. 6:1). It yields fruit in varying degrees of abundance—in a hundredfold, sixtyfold, and thirtyfold. This indicates that although all good soils receive the same good seed, the harvest varies. The limitation is not from the seed; it is from the soil. We should never assume that we are already getting the most harvest out of God's Word in our heart. There's always *so much more* in God.

> *God's Word is the wind beneath the wings of faith.*

The Word kept the centurion's servant from dying (Matt. 8:5–13); raised the unburied corpse of the widow of Nain's son (Luke 7:11–17); and raised the buried, putrid Lazarus from the dead (John 11:1–44). In a sense, the Word yielded thirtyfold, sixtyfold, and a hundredfold, as the occasions demanded.

If we stop pressing ahead in our walk with God, our harvest ends. We should always lift our cups to heaven to be filled by the incessant flow from above. As long as our cups are up, God will never stop pouring into them. May we never stop seeking His face for more harvest in our lives. If we can get a hundredfold, why settle for less?

THE SEED IS NEVER THE PROBLEM

It is important to emphasize that the seed is never the problem. If there's a problem, it's with the soil. The seed is always perfect; yet its environment can incapacitate it, as we have clearly seen from this parable. Teaching the truth is not enough; we must create an enabling environment for the truth to thrive. For example, teaching our children or church members the truth but carelessly exposing them to temptations may incapacitate the Word in their lives. Even Jesus taught us to pray thus: "And do not lead us into temptation, but deliver us from the evil one" (Matt. 6:13).

> *The good soil is not an accident of nature. It is intentionally tilled, even ploughed, to prepare for the seed.*

Birds are always present whenever seeds are sown. Therefore, preachers should fortify themselves and their audiences with prayer to ward off the evil birds ready to snatch away the good seed before it gets the chance to take root. Removal of thorns should be a continuous exercise. Since life is full of thorns, we must continuously weed out the thorns that are competing with the Word of God in our heart. Can your heart be tilled by correction, admonishment, and instructions? An untilled heart cannot produce great harvests.

The proof of our salvation is not just our zeal, but also our consistency. Of what use is it if we spring up too quickly, only to wither in the heat of the day? To be fruitful, we must remain faithful to the very end (Matt. 24:13). We need to be deeply rooted in the Word if we hope to endure to the end.

THE GENEROSITY OF THE SOWER

Finally, let's talk about the generosity of God. Knowing that the seeds may not grow to fruition, He still gave each soil a chance. "But God demonstrates His own love towards us, in that while we were still sinners, Christ died for us" (Rom. 5:8). He didn't spare His only Son. He gave His best to the world, and many keep rejecting His gift—yet He is not deterred by our ingratitude and rejection.

> *Can your heart be tilled by correction, admonishment, and instructions? An untilled heart cannot yield its best.*

God has done His part by giving us the seed. We must do our part by receiving it and ensuring that it finds a conducive environment in our hearts. The Word can be for our salvation or as a witness to our refusal (Matt. 24:14). It's time to

> plant the good seeds of righteousness, and you will harvest a crop of love. Plow up the hard ground of your hearts, for now is the time to seek the LORD, that He may come and shower righteousness upon you. (Hos. 10:12 NLT)

Chapter 7

THE GROWING SEED

ჱჱჱჱჱჱჱჱჱჱ

Jesus also said, "The Kingdom of God is like a farmer who scatters seed on the ground. Night and day, while he's asleep or awake, the seed sprouts and grows, but he does not understand how it happens. The earth produces the crops on its own. First a leaf blade pushes through, then the heads of wheat are formed, and finally the grain ripens. And as soon as the grain is ready, the farmer comes and harvests it with a sickle, for the harvest time has come."

MARK 4:26–29 (NLT)

In the previous chapter, we discussed the parable of the sower. The current parable zooms in on one of its key elements: the seed. While the parable of the sower is focused on the condition of the soil on which the seed fell, the parable of the growing seed takes a deeper look at the growth process of the seed itself. The former parable gives us the beginning (sowing) and end (harvest or failure) of the process, but it skips the middle details of the dynamics and timeline of the seed growth process. The current parable fills that gap.

These two parables, when combined, give us an in-depth insight into the key components of evangelism (the 3 s's of evangelism): the sower, the seed, and the soil. The sower, God, works through His servants (the believers) to plant the seed, His Word. The soil symbolizes the human heart, which we've *dissected* in the previous chapter.

We will now focus on the seed, which for this analysis has been extended to also represent God's will and purpose for our lives, as these are important components of His kingdom. We will consider the act of sowing seeds, the discipline involved, and the dynamics of seed growth.

DILIGENCE IN SOWING

After the destructive deluge had receded, Noah offered a sweet-smelling sacrifice to God. On smelling the aroma, God was pleased, and He promised to never again curse the ground because of humans, even though every inclination of the human heart is evil from childhood (Gen. 8:21). He also promised that "while the earth remains, seedtime and harvest, cold and heat, and summer and winter, and day and night shall not cease" (Gen. 8:22). This is a covenant that will last as long as the earth remains.

The subsistence of all humanity has hinged on this promise through the ages. What do the stone age, bronze age, iron age, industrial age, jet age, and the information age have in common? Humans, space, and time, obviously, but food is a strong contender. With all our technological advances, we still haven't outgrown the need for food.

Even before the development of agriculture, humans lived as nomadic hunter-gatherers who depended on fruit and wild progenitors of crops, such as barley, peas, and wheat. With agriculture comes the switch from nomadic living to more permanent settlements and farming. Civilizations formed around reliable food supply, either home-grown or imported from other regions. Without this assurance from God, it is safe to say there wouldn't be any civilizations, or even life at all.

> *The 3 s's of evangelism are: the sower, the seed, and the soil.*

Agriculture is one of the many examples of man collaborating with God to achieve specific goals. Humans do the work of ploughing the field, planting the seed, and watering the crop, while God gives the increase. For all human effort, nothing grows without the blessing of God. This is not to encourage indolence or fatalism that makes us throw up our hands in resignation while muttering *que será, será* (what will be, will be).

Since God has promised to bless the work of our hands (Deut. 28:12), we cannot afford to be lazy or throw our responsibilities back at Him. If we do nothing, there will be nothing for God to bless. Simple mathematics shows that:

$$0^{1000} = 0$$

$$1^{1000} = 1$$

$$1.1^{1000} = 2.47 \times 10^{41}$$

What a difference a tenth makes! It generated a massive increase from one to almost a tredecillion (a trillion has 12 zeros, while a tredecillion has 42 zeros).

The base number is the human input, while the exponent (or power) is God's grace upon our input. The same level of grace doesn't always yield the same level of output. For example, nations with comparable natural resources do not always have similar levels of prosperity—in this sense, the human input is often the factor that makes the difference.

What we often term *blessing* is the output of the multiplier effect of God's grace acting on human input. Hence, we need to add diligence to our faith to produce astounding results. Notice how Apostle Paul acted diligently to ensure that the grace upon his life yielded the maximum result:

> But by the grace of God I am what I am, and His grace towards me was not in vain; *but I labored more abundantly than they all*, yet not I, but the grace of God which was with me. (1 Cor. 15:10, emphasis mine)

But we can also veer off to the other extreme of *all effort and no grace*. When many people find themselves in a rut, rather than seek God's face to evaluate their lives and ferret out the cause of their problems, they simply double their effort. It's like spinning the wheels of a car stuck fast in mud. You may end up ruining the car and exhausting yourself as you sink deeper into the rut—with the dirt of your frustration sent flying in all directions. When God's grace is missing, whatever effort one puts in comes to essentially the same thing: little or nothing.

$$100^{0} = 10000^{0} = 1000000^{0} = 1$$

Unless the LORD builds the house, they labor in vain who build it; unless the LORD guards the city, the watchman stays awake in vain. It is vain for you to rise up early, to sit up late, to eat the bread of sorrows; for so He gives His beloved sleep. (Psa. 127:1–2)

TRAINING FOR THE MISSION

While God won't assent to ventures outside of His will, His approved will may be delayed or aborted in a particular life because of human failure or negligence. Ultimately, God's desire will be done, but the *vessel* for its fulfillment may be changed. The fate of Samson and Prophet Eli readily comes to mind. Though approved by God for great things, they both fell short and had their missions aborted. At a national scale, the men of Judah, despite having God with them, failed to drive out the people living in parts of the land God had promised them.

> The LORD was with the men of Judah. They took possession of the hill country, but they were unable to drive the people from the plains because they had chariots fitted with iron. (Judg. 1:19 NIV)

The Israelites couldn't drive out the people of the plains because the latter had a superior technology—their chariots were fitted with iron. God could have given Israel total victory despite their inferior technology. After all, there are several records of miraculous battle victories in the Bible. But God doesn't just give us victory, He also teaches our hands to war. "Blessed be the LORD my Rock, who trains my hands for war, and my fingers for battle" (Psa. 144:1). In fact, God allowed some foreign nations to remain in the Promised Land to train the Israelites in the acts of war (Judg. 3:1–3)—He didn't make all their enemies disappear.

The initial setback the men of Judah experienced would have prompted them to engage their God-given brains in developing superior weapons of war—that is, God was training their hands for war and their fingers for battle. The result of this training became readily apparent during the reign of King Uzziah, about whom the Bible says:

> Uzziah provided shields, spears, helmets, coats of armor, bows and slingstones for the entire army. And he made devices in

Jerusalem, invented by skillful men, to be on the towers and the corners, to shoot arrows and large stones. So, his fame spread far and wide, for he was marvellously helped till he became strong. (2 Chr. 26:14–15)

God *can* give us jobs for which we are not qualified. But *will* He always do that? With time, what will that make us? More diligent or plain lazy? What sort of a father would God be if He encourages such irresponsibility? He would rather train our hands and fingers to acquire the skills requisite for the job.

God can do the miracle of granting us victory without us lifting a finger, but He often marvellously helps us till we become strong like King Uzziah by training our fingers for battle. That initial rejection during the job application doesn't mean God is not with us. It may be a wake-up call for training our hands and fingers to upscale our skills and qualifications.

The purpose of God's miracles and providence is not to encourage mediocrity or indolence. They are given to strengthen our faith in Him and to show us He rules in the affairs of men and has power over everyone and everything, even the winds and the sea (Matt. 8:27). He loves us and can rescue us from seemingly hopeless situations. This assurance should energize us to boldly pursue our God-given dreams—that is, to diligently sow our seed.

As recorded in the Bible, God parted River Jordan miraculously a few times; for example, for Joshua and the Israelites (Josh. 3:14–17); Prophet Elijah and Elisha (2 Kings 2:8–9); and Prophet Elisha (2 Kings 2:14). However, God did not allow the miraculous parting of River Jordan to become the standard mode of transportation for the Israelites. Through the years, they crossed River Jordan thousands of times—without miracles. They simply learned how to build boats. Even Jesus crossed River Jordan several times (Matt. 19:1; Mark 10:1)—in boats.

> **But God doesn't just give us victory, He also teaches our hands to war.**

This may explain why many apparently religious and prayerful nations struggle with widespread poverty and other vices. Besides not living up to the truth of the faith they ostentatiously profess, they often leave to God what He has equipped them to manage. They fail to understand that one of God's blessings is the ability to acquire skills and develop their human resources. Instead of working together with God, they expect Him to do everything for them. They are waiting for Him, while He is waiting for them.

THE DYNAMICS OF SEED GROWTH

Five phases of seed growth are presented in this parable: *seed, leaf blade, heads of wheat, ripening grain,* and *ready grain.* Once the seed has been successfully sown in a good soil, God gives the increase, but not necessarily in the manner we anticipate or within our expected time frame.

For a while, it seems like the sown seed is dead and buried. We are often eager to see positive responses as soon as the gospel is preached. We may easily become discouraged if we do not get a positive reaction from the sinner, or if we are faced with a negative one. Yet though the seed is buried, it's neither dead nor forgotten.

The Holy Spirit works silently through the sown Word. If we lose faith in God's ability to grow the seed at this stage, we may lean on our own understanding and arms of flesh, which will surely fail us. We may be tempted to dig up the seed to see what is wrong, when actually nothing is wrong, except our impatience.

Many parents easily fall into this trap. They become impatient at the apparent absence of *any sign of life* in their children, and they begin to use either threat or inducement. We cannot win a spiritual battle with physical weapons. Let us learn from the germination of the physical seed, which doesn't always need our help, and trust God to grow the spiritual seed as well.

> They fail to understand that one of God's blessings is the ability to acquire skills ...

While we think nothing is happening, the unseen seed is quietly pushing against the might of the soil resting on it. It is finding pores through which to penetrate. It grows, against all odds, until it breaks through the soil surface—at the appointed time.

A leaf blade finally emerges through the otherwise bare soil surface. This brings us some encouragement. When an errant child shows some sign of remorse, it fills the parents' hearts with joy. We can compare this sign to a leaf blade emerging through the hard, crusted soil surface. The change didn't begin on the day we noticed it; it's been some *days* in the making. We may still be skeptical at this stage: Is this leaf from the seed we planted or is it just a weed? After all, we are not the only ones sowing seeds into the person's life. What if it's just a gimmick to get something from us?

The next phase of growth clears our doubt. The heads of wheat are formed. We now see clear signs of repentance: conviction of sin, of righteousness, and of judgment. "And when He [Holy Spirit] has come, He will convict the world of sin, and of righteousness, and of judgment" (John 16:8). The sinner repents and actively seeks forgiveness. The convert thirsts for God, even though he may not be able to articulate his feelings or know how to satisfy his thirst.

In time, the grain ripens. The believer is mature and doing great exploits in God's kingdom, including dispersing the seed of the Word as the wind of the Holy Spirit blows across the field. The ripening grain stays on the farm doing great works until the farmer deems it fit and ready to be harvested and stored safely in the barn.

FINALLY, THE HARVEST!

Harvest signifies the removal and collection of the crops (souls) from the field (the world) into the barn, which is the kingdom of God. In a sense, both heaven and the universal church make up the kingdom of God. Heaven hosts the *church triumphant*, while the earth hosts the *church militant*.

The church triumphant is composed of all the saints who have *slept* in the Lord, while the church militant comprises all the living saints on earth who struggle as soldiers of Christ against sin, Satan, the world, and the flesh. Thus, the harvest is the relocation of souls from the world into the church—either into the church triumphant (through death and Rapture) or into the church militant (through evangelism and conversion).

> *The purpose of God's miracles and providence is not to encourage mediocrity or indolence.*

Both interpretations are supported by the Scripture. Concerning the harvest into the church militant, Jesus, while explaining to His disciples that His *food* was to do God's will and finish His assignment, said,

You know the saying, "Four months between planting and harvest." But I say, wake up and look around. The fields are already ripe for harvest. ... I sent you to harvest where you didn't plant; others had already done the work, and now you will get to gather the harvest. (John 4:35,38 NLT)

Regarding the harvest into the church triumphant, Jesus said the following in the parable of the weeds:

Let both grow together until the harvest. Then I will tell the harvesters to sort out the weeds, tie them into bundles, and burn them, and to put the wheat in the barn. (Matt. 13:30 NLT)

From the two Bible passages above, we see that the saints of God on earth handle the harvest into the church militant, while the angels of God handle the harvest into the church triumphant. When the mature believer's time of harvest into the church triumphant arrives, the angels of God receive and usher his soul into eternity with God.

What we often term *premature death* has more to do with purpose than with age. Premature death signifies the abortion of one's purpose and destiny, regardless of the age at death. We humans number our days in *chronos* (clock time or calendar years), while God numbers them in *kairos* (God's appointed time for a specific purpose—the opportune time). *Chronos* is the time we count; *kairos* is the time that counts. One measure of an impactful life is the number of *kairos* moments realized within our *chronos* days.

> *While you think nothing is happening, the unseen seed is quietly pushing against the might of the soil resting on it.*

Kairos is often depicted in classical literature as a young man on tiptoe, with a pair of wings behind each foot, a lock of hair flowing into his face, and the back of his head bald. His youthfulness depicts his agility, which coupled with his tiptoeing, makes it easy for him to elude us. The wings on his feet signify the lightning speed with which an opportune time can metamorphose into a missed opportunity. The hair lock flowing into his face and the baldness of the back of his head indicate the dangers of lack of foresight and preparation. We must seize our opportune time with adequate preparation; that is, we must grab the hair lock. Once he passes us by, it is difficult, if not impossible, to grab him by the slick bald back of his head.

When we have lived and fulfilled all of God's purposes for our lives, we have fulfilled the number of our days in the sight of God—regardless of our age. We are deemed a *ready* grain at that point. Harvest of anything other than the ready grain can be considered premature death.

Saul, the first king of ancient Israel, suffered a premature death even though he died as a grandpa with a five-year-old grandson (2 Sam. 4:4). He aborted his life's purpose through disobedience, jealousy, lies, failure to accept responsibility for his faults, and vindictiveness. He didn't fulfill God's purpose for his life, and he ultimately died ingloriously, surrounded by ruthless enemies (1 Sam. 31:3–6).

> *Chronos is the time we count; kairos is the time that counts. One measure of an impactful life is the number of kairos moments realized within our chronos days.*

In contrast, Stephen, a church deacon and the first Christian martyr, did not die prematurely even though he never saw his fortieth birthday. As he was being stoned to death, he had none other than Jesus Christ Himself standing at the right hand of God to welcome him home.

Both King Saul and Stephen were surrounded by their enemies in their last moments, but the latter had heaven standing in anticipation of his arrival. Saul—the tall, handsome, and once powerful king—killed himself to escape shame and torture. Indeed, how the mighty have fallen!

A person may die in her eighties but have only *lived* for forty years. Such a person has suffered stunted growth. She's stuck at either the *leaf blade* or the *heads of wheat stage*. Of such people, the Bible says,

> In fact, though by this time you ought to be teachers, you need someone to teach you the elementary truths of God's word all over again. You need milk, not solid food! (Heb. 5:12)

It is God's desire for us to grow into maturity. May we receive the grace to grow and thrive in the Lord's vineyard.

If we live well, once is enough. We will have no need for extra time, even if that were possible. At the end of our lives, we can boldly say like Paul, "I have fought the good fight, I have finished the race, I have kept the faith" (2 Tim. 4:7). From that point on in Paul's life, it no longer mattered when he would die. It was never going to be a premature death.

Paul, a *ripe* and *ready* grain, kept edifying the church even though he had fulfilled his life's purpose. At a point, he was torn between being harvested into heaven and staying longer in the field for the sake of the church:

> For I am hard-pressed between the two, having a desire to depart and be with Christ, which is far better. Nevertheless, to remain in the flesh is more needful for you. (Phil. 1:23–24)

This is not to encourage believers to desire or vigorously pursue early death. After all, one can die young without fulfilling purpose. We should trust God to bless us with long lives here on earth, but what is more important is to ensure we live every day with a sense of purpose. If it pleases God to leave us in the field into our old age, our testimony can still be like those of whom the Bible says,

> They shall still bring forth fruit in old age; they shall be fat and flourishing; to shew that the LORD is upright: He is my rock, and there is no unrighteousness in Him. (Psa. 92:14–15 KJV)

SOWING IN PARTNERSHIP WITH GOD

We have established that some ventures, such as agriculture, require collaborative effort between God and man. It is a great privilege to be invited by God to partner with Him on a project. Such is the case in this parable. God has invited us to partner with Him in spreading the Word of His Truth, the gospel. He can do it without us, yet He has chosen to do it with us. It is an honour and should be our pleasure to work as God's co-labourers in sowing the seed of the gospel anywhere He sends us.

However, it is easy to forget our place in this partnership—we are the junior partners. We often get so carried away by our effort that we forget it is still God who gives the increase and calls the shots.

Not only does He call the shots, but He also calls the shoots out of the ground.

Ministers of the gospel may get so worried and pine away over the condition of their flock, unsure whether their sermons are having the desired impact on the lives of their congregants. While the limitations inherent in our language may make us speak in certain manners, we should never forget that these are not strictly *our* sermons; they are *His* sermons. Similarly, the people are not ours; they are His.

This understanding, even if not always obvious in our speech, can lift off our shoulders burdens that are not ours to bear. Paul plants, Apollos waters, but it is God who gives the increase (1 Cor. 3:6). Our assignments include sitting at the Master's feet until we get the right seeds, diligently and wisely spreading the seeds, and watering them. What is *not* in our job description is bringing about or understanding the mystery of seed growth and multiplication. That is God's job.

Instead of fretting over how the seeds will grow, let our sweat and tears go into sowing the right seeds and watering them. That way, we save ourselves needless heartaches and pains. For even when the farmer sleeps, the kingdom of God still grows (Mark 4:27). *Sleep* as used in this parable does not indicate negligence or slothfulness. It simply implies attendance to other legitimate issues of life. That the crop grows without the farmer's intervention

> *Premature death signifies the abortion of one's purpose and destiny, regardless of the age at death.*

means God can accomplish His purposes even when we are absent or unaware of what He is doing. He only needs us to faithfully deliver the seeds He has committed into our hands.

Are you worried about the best way to raise your children in this perverse world? Why not focus on sowing the seed of the Word into their lives? And follow it up with prayers and encouragement. God will ensure its growth, even when you are not around them.

Just as a farmer cannot force a seed to grow, we cannot force spiritual growth on others. You can beat a child into the church, but you cannot beat the church into the child. "For the wrath of man does not produce the righteousness of God" (James 1:20). We should avoid the temptation of taking over people's lives in an apparent bid to take them to heaven *whether they like it or not*. We cannot take anyone to heaven against their will. That's the reason the term *Whoever wills* is very common in the Bible. It is the Word that is hidden (sown) in the heart—not threat or inducement—that makes a person refrain from sinning against God (Psa. 119:11).

When children go off to college is not when we begin to pay close attention to their spiritual health. That's almost twenty years too late. Let's start sowing the seed of the Word into their tender hearts even when they appear too young to understand. The world does not wait for their consent (or ours) before it indoctrinates them, whether actively or subtly—and neither should we. It's our responsibility to fill their hearts with the Word as early as possible. We water the sown seed with prayers, encouragement, and modelling the Word in our own lives.

Remember, even when the seed is out of your sight and hands, it is still safe in God's sight and hands. His hands are bigger than yours, and His eyes are also sharper than yours. So, rest in your God. He can take care of everything better than you can. In fact, your feeling of helplessness or weakness can be your strength, if it drives you to God in prayer. It is He who "gives strength to the weary and increases the power of the weak" (Isa. 40:29 NIV). When you feel inadequate, remember God is saying to you, "My grace is sufficient for you, for My strength is made perfect in weakness" (2 Cor. 12:9).

> *Instead of fretting over how the seeds will grow, let our sweat and tears go into sowing the right seeds and watering them.*

WAITING FOR THE WORLD TO CHANGE

Ours is a busy world with barely any room for anything that doesn't bring tangible benefits to us. We commit many hours to furthering our careers, making money, or having fun. However, we seem to have little motivation to reach out to others with the gospel of Christ. At intervals, we observe the evil going on around us and complain about how bad the world has become. Yet the solution to the world's problems is in our heart and mouth—it is the gospel.

We indict ourselves anytime we complain about the world, if we are not actively engaged in evangelism. We are like a man holding the key to a fully stocked but locked grain silo complaining that the people around him are dying of hunger. We find it easier to discuss our favourite sporting events, politics, and current affairs, but we struggle to share our faith with others or even share tracts. If people would call on the Lord, He is able and willing to save and deliver them. But

> how then shall they call on Him in whom they have not believed? And how shall they believe in Him of whom they have not heard? And how shall they hear without a preacher? And how shall they preach, except they be sent? (Rom. 10:14–15)

Every believer has been sent to preach the gospel, even to the ends of the earth (Mark 16:15). We don't need a special invitation to go preach; we already have the Great Commission. The mandate and responsibility to preach is on all of us. What may differ is the specific group to which God has sent us. He sent some specifically to children or teenagers, while He sent others to adults or geriatrics.

This specific call does not mean we cannot, or should not, preach to anyone outside of our core target group when we have the opportunity. It simply means we have been specially equipped to connect better with our target group. Many great preachers who do well with adults may struggle to hold the attention of children or teenagers. The same children may listen with rapt attention when the minister *sent* to them is ministering to them.

> *The world does not wait for their consent (or ours) before it indoctrinates them, whether actively or subtly—and neither should we.*

It's not just a matter of *whom*, but also a matter of *where*. God has sent some to preach on Wall Street, while He has equipped others for mission in obscure villages in jungles barely touched by civilization. It's important we all seek God's face to know where and to whom He desires to send us.

Once we are clear on the *whom* and *where*, the next step is the *how*. We need to ask for courage and wisdom to know how to go about executing the Great Commission in our niche and to our target audience. Have you been sent to children? There are creative ways to engage them with the gospel. It could be the creation of godly cartoons, comics, songs, Bibles for children, Christian camps, Scripture candies, games, apps, book reading, or short stories. The list is endless. For example, a family tired of complaining and debating whether Christians should take part in Halloween celebrations decided to hand out Scripture candies and cookies (with Scriptures written on the wraps) to the children seeking treats. In a sense, they handed out *sweet tracts*.

Stop complaining. Ask God for wisdom on how best to preach the gospel where He has sent you. The thicker the darkness, the greater the need for light. Cursing the darkness is of little use; it's much better to be the light.

OPPOSITION TO THE GOSPEL

Regardless of our creativity and wisdom in sharing the gospel, opposition will surely arise. That is why we need courage. Without boldness, we will fizzle out and start making excuses for not preaching. We may even be tempted to settle for the *live and let live* philosophy.

A major challenge with this philosophy is that the devil does not believe in it. We may end up like a pugilist who sets all the rules for a bout against an opponent who doesn't respect the rules. If our opponent comes with guns and grenades, it is foolishness to assume he won't use them simply because *we* won't use them. The opponent may not follow our *hands only* rule. We must protect ourselves.

> *We indict ourselves anytime we complain about the world, if we are not actively engaged in evangelism.*

Similarly, the devil never stops pushing our boundaries, even if we choose not to push his. If we fail to preach the gospel, the devil doesn't leave us and our children alone. He starts preaching his own doctrines and ideologies to them as soon as they come out of the womb.

It is a dynamic equilibrium, not a static one. If we don't hold our ground, the devil will push us back and dispossess us of our land. However, we don't stand our ground through physical violence or unrest. Rather, we raid the devil's camp through fervent prayers and evangelism powered by the Holy Spirit.

> For the weapons of our warfare are not carnal but mighty in God for pulling down strongholds, casting down arguments and every high thing that exalts itself against the knowledge of God, bringing every thought into captivity to the obedience of Christ, and being ready to punish all disobedience when your obedience is fulfilled. (2 Cor. 10:4–6)

Chapter 8

THE WEEDS

Here is another story Jesus told: "The Kingdom of Heaven is like a farmer who planted good seed in his field. But that night as the workers slept, his enemy came and planted weeds among the wheat, then slipped away. When the crop began to grow and produce grain, the weeds also grew. The farmer's workers went to him and said, 'Sir, the field where you planted that good seed is full of weeds! Where did they come from?' 'An enemy has done this!' the farmer exclaimed. 'Should we pull out the weeds?' they asked. 'No,' he replied, 'you'll uproot the wheat if you do. Let both grow together until the harvest. Then I will tell the harvesters to sort out the weeds, tie them into bundles, and burn them, and to put the wheat in the barn.'"

MATTHEW 13:24–30 (NLT)

This is yet another parable related to seeds told by Jesus to explain the concept of the kingdom of God. Other similar parables include the parables of the sower, the growing seed, and the mustard seed. While these other parables deal with the condition of the soil, the dynamics of seed growth, and the fate of the seeds, the current parable focuses on the co-existence of the good seeds with the bad ones. In this parable, the seeds represent human agents.

NO ACCIDENT OF NATURE

How do weeds get into farms originally sown with good seeds (wheat in this parable)? After all, it is rare for a farmer to intentionally sow weeds along with good seeds. Weeds seem to have a mind of their own, and they often simply take root and overrun a field without needing the farmer's help. Their seeds are typically dispersed by wind, water, farm equipment, animals, or people passing by. However, in this parable, Jesus made it clear that the weeds were intentionally planted by an enemy.

In an agrarian society, such sabotage is not unheard of. A saboteur may maliciously spread weed seeds on the target farm. In such instances, a weed bearing some semblance to the crop is introduced to the farm to masquerade the sabotage until the damage has been done. By the time the farmer realizes that weeds are growing alongside his wheat, it is often too late.

It is often at maturity that the differences between the two plants become pronounced. While the wheat produces harvestable edibles, the weed does not yield any produce of value to the farmer. But it is worse than that. The weeds were not planted merely to fool the farmer into overestimating his harvest. In this parable, the primary purpose of the weeds was to wreak havoc on the wheat. So, not only do weeds occupy the space meant for the wheat, they also often outcompete the wheat for resources and may infest them with pests and diseases.

Some have proposed that this parable is an illustration of the condition of the church, with the wheat representing true believers and the weed representing false believers (mere professors). While it is not in doubt that there are true and false believers in the church, this parable is not intended to address such challenges. Rather, it is focused on the relentless assault mounted on the church (the wheat) by the world (the weed).

Jesus identified the main characters in the parable in verses 37–39 of the same chapter. He identified the good farmer as Himself, the field as the world, the good seed as the believers, the weeds as the unbelievers, the sower of the weeds as Satan, the harvest as the end of the world, and the harvesters as the angels.

A lesson of note in this parable is the intentionality of planting both the wheat and the weeds. Nothing in God's kingdom happens by accident. The farmer intentionally planted and maintained the wheat for his profit. Similarly, the enemy intentionally planted the weeds to hurt the wheat, frustrate the farmer, and reduce the harvest.

In reality, the enemy didn't particularly care for the wheat. His target had always been the farmer. The wheat was just a means through which he would assail the farmer. He was like an evil man trying to sleep with the wife of his business rival, just to spite and humiliate him. He may not care in the least for the woman, but his eyes are on the target, the husband. The wife, like the wheat, is nothing more than a means to an end for the enemy, who may seduce her and shower her with so much *affection* to make her fall out of love with her husband and fall in love with him. Yet unbeknownst to her, she is nothing more than a pawn in his evil game.

> *Nothing in God's kingdom happens by accident.*

But neither did the enemy care for the weeds. The weeds are just convenient tools serving as his—to use the common political term—*useful idiots* for assailing the wheat and, ultimately, the farmer. Thus, no matter the *affection* Satan appears to shower on humans, he doesn't really care about us. He is only bent on thwarting the purposes of God by making us fall short of His glory.

Amazed at the glory God has conferred on man, the Psalmist said:

> What is man that You are mindful of him, and the son of man that You visit him? For You have made him a little lower than the angels, and You have crowned him with glory and honor. (Psa. 8:4–5)

But the Psalmist was not the only one in awe of this phenomenon called *man*, a being made in God's image and likeness and commanded to have dominion on earth. The devil is also astonished and can't stop wondering what is so special about man that makes God care so much for him. Isn't he just a despicable puny little creature? Yet God has crowned him with glory and honour.

God has given to man the glory and honour the devil has always coveted. Expectedly, the devil isn't going to take it lying down; he's committed to destroying man. He is probably thinking: "What a travesty! Man must be destroyed! God must be humiliated for humiliating me this way!" His thought process is revealed in the book of Isaiah where he said,

I will ascend into heaven, I will exalt my throne above the stars of God; I will also sit on the mount of the congregation on the farthest sides of the north. (Isa. 14:13)

Following his failed attempt to seize God's throne in a celestial coup d'état, he was forced to become terrestrial and has since been relentlessly pursuing any victories, including enthroning himself over humanity and sabotaging God's plans and purposes on earth.

God remains his ultimate target for humiliation and frustration. Man is just a means to achieving his goal. Hence, anytime we are faced with temptation from the devil, even in our closet, we should appreciate the significance of the moment. It is far more crucial than our individual selves. At that moment, we are at the centre of a cosmic battle: Satan wants to humiliate God by turning us, His choice creation, against Him in sin.

Sin is an affront to God's holiness and dignity. It is falling short of His glory which He has conferred upon us to the chagrin of the devil. What better way to honour God than to obey Him right in the devil's face? Whenever we overcome a temptation, God smiles in admiration, while the devil cries in shame. Even in times of intense trials, like Job's, God is delighted and glorified in His faithful children.

The Bible says, "Do not bring shame on the name of your God by using it to swear falsely. I am the LORD" (Lev. 19:12 NLT). Yet swearing falsely is not the only sin that brings reproach to the name of the Lord; in fact, every sin does. When we continually yield to sin, we become its slave, and the devil sneers at the ability of our God to keep us safe from sin and evil. We risk becoming like the Israelites concerning whom God said,

But when they were scattered among the nations, they brought shame on my holy name. For the nations said, "These are the people of the LORD, but he couldn't keep them safe in his own land!" (Ezek. 36:20 NLT)

Our God is able to keep us from sin and present us faultless in His glory (Jude 24). But if we fall into sin, we should repent and believe that Christ, our Advocate, has washed us clean, restored us, and endued us with the power to say no to sin (1 John 2:1). By His grace, sin will not have dominion over us (Rom. 6:14).

THE SNEAKY DEVIL

Once the enemy planted the weeds, he slipped away from the farm. The enemy is often sneaky in his attack on the believer, be it in the family, church, or society. He acts in a manner reminiscent of the Amalekites, who sneaked up and attacked the Israelites from the rear, rather than engaging them in direct combat. They strategically attacked the vulnerable, exhausted, and feeble individuals who could not keep up with the rest of the group (Deut. 25:17–18). They must have learned this strategy from the devil himself.

The devil is a sneaky spoiler. He's so sneaky that we rarely see his footprint. So, we accuse each other of planting the weeds. For example, a husband may accuse his wife of causing the issues in their marriage, and the wife pays him back in equal measure, or even more. All the while, the sneaky enemy is laughing his head off behind the scenes.

Unfortunately, many of us are more concerned about winning arguments and apportioning blames than getting rid of the weeds and repairing the broken hedge through which the enemy slipped in. We fail to realize that unless we deal with the sneaky enemy, even if we win the arguments, we'll still ultimately lose.

When I was younger, the modus operandi of pickpockets in my neighbourhood was to get unsuspecting strangers distracted with flimsy arguments while their accomplices stole the strangers' wallets. Whether or not the strangers won the arguments didn't matter. They still ended up losing. They either won the argument but lost their wallets, or they lost both the argument and their wallets. It was a lose-lose game for the unwary strangers.

Similarly, for us, we may win many arguments but lose something far more valuable than the arguments. Why not focus on what matters? Why not fix our broken walls and keep the enemy at bay?

Until we fix the breach in our wall through which the enemy sneaks in, we cannot be rid of weeds. It's of little use to kill the serpent inside our barn while we leave unfixed the breach in the wall through which it crawled in. As long as the breach remains, more serpents will crawl in. Likewise, repairing our broken hedge keeps the sneaky enemy away and reduces the influx of weeds.

The enemy sneaked in while the farm workers were sleeping, probably after a hard day's work. The devil often sneaks in when we are tired, even if it is from legitimate business of the day. Sometimes, after a hard-won victory, we may be caught off guard in our relaxed state. "We should therefore be sober and vigilant because our adversary the devil walks about like a roaring lion, seeking whom he may devour" (1 Pet. 5:8).

A GOOD GOD, YET EVIL ALL AROUND. MAKE IT MAKE SENSE

"Master, did you not sow good seed in your field? How then does it have weeds?"These questions are familiar to us but are often presented in other formats. A common way the questions are phrased is: If God is so good and mighty, why is there so much evil in the world?

The Jews of Jesus' day were under Roman rule and expected the Messiah to liberate them. Not only that, but He would also free them from all sorts of evils. When Jesus rode into Jerusalem on a donkey, the people adoringly screamed out in anticipation of their deliverance, "Hosannah!" which can be translated as "Please save us now!" (Matt. 21:9).

They were expecting the Messiah to save them from the Romans, not from their sins. However, Jesus seemed to have no interest in leading an uprising against the Romans. He even told them,

> My Kingdom is not of this world. If My kingdom were of this world, My servants would fight, so that I should not be delivered to the Jews; but now My kingdom is not from here. (John 18:36)

Jesus did not stop the Romans, and neither did He stop His own concocted arrest. In fact, to the people's disappointment, the Messiah who was expected to liberate them from the Romans ended up being crucified by the same Romans. From their perspective, Jesus fell significantly short of their expectations for a Messiah: "At least if you can't save us, try to save yourself, man."

Even His disciples were initially confused about the nature of His kingdom. He had to keep emphasizing to them that His kingdom was not of this world. He kept reminding them that the prophecies described Him as the *suffering Messiah* who would be persecuted and ultimately killed (Psa. 22 and Isa. 53).

Jesus didn't come to depose Caesar or destroy the Romans. Neither did He come to swiftly eradicate all the evils in the world. He came to transform the world—yes, but one heart at a time. Thus, the change must start from the inside, as powered by the Holy Spirit. A time will come when evil will be eradicated, but that wasn't going to be at Jesus' first coming.

It will be at His second coming, after the blowing of the seventh trumpet in the book of Revelation. Then we will all triumphantly say, "The kingdoms of this world have become the kingdoms of our Lord and of His Christ, and He shall reign forever and ever!" (Rev. 11:15). In the meantime, the weeds and the wheat must co-exist. Evil and good will co-exist in the world until the final whistle is blown.

Weeds compete with wheat for nutrients, water, and space. They often harbour pests and diseases dangerous to wheat and can ultimately reduce crop yield. The weeds are hurtful to the wheat, both by temptation and persecution, just as Paul said in his allegory in the book of Galatians, "But, as he who was born according to the flesh persecuted him who was born according to the Spirit, even so it is now" (Gal. 4:29).

So, why not remove the weeds immediately? God, in His infinite wisdom, has decided that the best course of action is to allow the weeds and wheat grow together, for the time being. "Let both grow together until the harvest" (Matt. 13:30). Thus, evil grows alongside the good until the return of Christ. God's main reason for allowing this collocated concurrent growth is to prevent the destruction of the wheat in the process of uprooting the weeds. "'Should we pull out the weeds?' they asked. 'No,' he replied, 'you'll uproot the wheat if you do'" (Matt. 13:28–29 NLT).

> *Sin is an affront to God's holiness and dignity. It is falling short of His glory which He has conferred upon us to the chagrin of the devil.*

His workers, like many of us, were eager to uproot the weeds and rid the world of all evils. But were they discerning enough to identify the weeds and skillful enough to uproot them without damaging the wheat? The farmer did not think so, "for we know in part" (1 Cor. 13:9). Judgment is too crucial and final to be undermined and contaminated by our ignorance and incompetence in accurately judging human motive, character, and action.

There are several ways in which our limitations as humans make judging and uprooting the weeds a dangerous task above our pay grade. First, our assessments and judgments may not be accurate, but the damage we cause may be devastating and irreversible.

Second, our limitations may make us misidentify slow-growing or strange-looking wheat as weed and destroy it. Some people's good works may not be readily visible to us, and we may incorrectly judge them as weeds deserving of destruction. Furthermore, there is a possibility of causing harm to immature or young Christians who are still in the process of growth and do not meet our expectations.

> *Jesus didn't come to depose Caesar or destroy the Romans. Neither did He come to swiftly eradicate all the evils in the world. He came to transform the world—yes, but one heart at a time.*

Third, we may soon become bitter. It is quite common to see people become the evil they set out to fight. Evil has tentacles which shoot out toxins that contaminate and infect people, even the people fighting it. Confronting evil without continuous fortification by the Holy Spirit is more dangerous than many believers realize. King David was probably alluding to this phenomenon when he summarized his life experiences in his last words thus:

> But the sons of Belial shall be all of them as thorns thrust away, because they cannot be taken with hands: But the man that shall touch them must be fenced with iron and the staff of a spear; and they shall be utterly burned with fire in the same place. (2 Sam. 23:6–7 KJV)

Fourth and closely related to the third point, we may not know when to stop. We may start out well but get increasingly incensed until our focus shifts from growing the wheat to routing the weeds.

Fifth, we don't know what issues people have already settled with God. We often judge people based on our knowledge of their past, but what if they have made their peace with God? Do we always know that?

Sixth, our zeal may be hijacked by the enemy to inflict pain on the world and the church. Saul's zeal for destroying the *weeds* contaminating his Jewish faith was hijacked by Satan and used to attack the true church of God. It took the humbling Damascus Road encounter for the veil to fall off his face.

Finally, the wheat and the weeds are so intertwined in this current age that any attempt to remove the weeds may lead to the premature removal of the wheat. For example, the removal of an ungodly parent may destroy the children; the removal of an ungodly employer may adversely affect his workers, even the godly ones; and the removal of ungodly doctors may adversely affect patients, even the pious ones.

Further, the premature removal of ungodly ministers who preach the truth but do not obey it may injure the young saints in their care. This brings up the question of how believers should deal with a preacher who preaches the truth of God's Word but doesn't obey it. Should Christians use the untoward lifestyle of a preacher as an excuse to discredit and disobey the truth he preaches?

The ideal minister exemplifies the truth he preaches. However, life is not always ideal, and people don't always have access to ideal ministers. When confronted with such circumstances, believers must prioritize the question of whether the preacher's words align with the truth. Though the preacher is in danger of destroying his own eternal destiny by living in disobedience, the listeners can still benefit from the truth he preaches. Concerning this suboptimal situation, Jesus said,

> So you must be careful to do everything they tell you. But do not do what they do, for they do not practice what they preach (Matt. 23:3 NLT)

HISTORICAL EXAMPLES HIGHLIGHTING THE DANGERS OF PREMATURE HARVESTING

We have previously discussed why it is best to leave the judgment or uprooting of the weeds to God. Now, we will look at some historical examples highlighting what happens when humans assume the role of God as the Judge. History is replete with such misadventures, but for the current discourse, time will only permit two examples: the Spanish Inquisition and Public Executions in Nigeria.

We should not confuse humans assuming the role of God as the ultimate Judge with the dispensation of justice by just, fair, and accountable governments of the land. After all, the Bible says,

Everyone must submit to governing authorities. For all authority comes from God, and those in positions of authority have been placed there by God. So, anyone who rebels against authority is rebelling against what God has instituted, and they will be punished. (Rom. 13:1–2 NLT)

We don't want to imagine the chaos that would ensue if good governance disappeared from the world suddenly, or more realistically, if it is eroded over time. However, despotic or corrupt governments defeat the purpose of governance. They miscarry justice and sell the poor for a loaf of bread. Concerning such corrupt leaders, the Bible says, "It is not good for a judge to take sides, but some will sin for only a piece of bread" (Prov. 28:21 New Century Version).

The Spanish Inquisition

The Spanish Inquisition,[1] which took place from 1478 to 1834, a period of about 350 years, is an example of how human attempt to usurp the place of God (as the Judge) and the angels (as harvesters) can go awry.

Taxation and discriminations targeted against non-Catholics in Europe had forced many Jews and Muslims to convert to Catholicism. Naturally, there were suspicions in some quarters that some conversions were all too convenient and were falsely done to avoid taxes and discrimination. The inquisition was inaugurated originally to sift from the true converts these *heretics*, *Crypto Jews* (secret Jews who were outwardly Christians but secretly practised Judaism) and other phony *new Christians* (conversos).

The accused on trial received either an acquittal, a penance, a reconciliation, or the most severe punishment known as *relaxation to the secular arm*. The accused relaxed to the secular arm, numbering in their thousands, were burned at the stake in a ritual of public penance known as *auto-da-fe*.

Some of the condemned repented publicly. The authorities garroted these individuals before burning their corpses, which was considered a merciful act compared to burning them alive. Some sources estimated that about 150,000 individuals were prosecuted during the Spanish Inquisition, and between 3,000 and 5,000 of them were executed.[2]

Public Executions in Nigeria

The second historical example happened in Nigeria immediately following the nation's civil war, also referred to as the Nigerian-Biafran war, spanning from July 6, 1967 to January 15, 1970. The country experienced a surge in armed robbery and violence as a result of the 30-month civil war, with unemployed soldiers and an excess supply of guns and ammunition contributing to this explosive situation. As a response to the increasing violence, the military junta took strict measures by introducing public execution as a deterrent for convicted criminals.

The country witnessed its first public execution on July 24, 1971.[3] The accused trio comprising of the infamous and stylish armed robber, Mr. Babatunde Folorunsho (also known as *Baba Oni Lace*, due to his love for extravagant lace attire, which he wore during robberies and subsequently his execution),[4] Joseph Ilobo, and Navy Sub-Lieutenant Williams Alders Oyazimo, were subjected to public execution at the Bar Beach in Lagos. Being the first of its kind in the country's history, a multitude of Nigerians flocked to the renowned beach out of sheer curiosity.

The condemned were tied to the stake, while the soldiers positioned themselves a short distance away, their guns primed and ready for action. At a point during the execution, one of the condemned, Joseph Ilobo, looked at the crowd and said, "Are all these people here to see me die? Ah! This is a wicked world ... I have not committed any crime."[5]

> Judgment is too crucial and final to be undermined and contaminated by our ignorance and incompetence in accurately judging human motive, character, and action.

When the military chaplain, Col. Pedro Martins, approached the condemned and asked them to pray for forgiveness, one of them, Sub-Lieutenant Oyazimo with a sob said, "[Revd.] Father, I am innocent. My blood will cleanse my family and my children will prosper."[6] Many Nigerians were deeply moved by his final words, which heightened their doubts about his guilt and raised suspicions that he had been falsely accused by fellow officers, possibly as a result of a personal grudge. Nevertheless, there is no evidence to substantiate the suspicion. Folorunsho, on his part, did not utter a word during his execution, and there was probably little sympathy for him as many people believed he had it coming to him.

The shots soon rang out and hot bullets pierced the restrained bodies of the condemned—guilty or not. The people celebrated the end of the notorious Folorunsho. However, their celebration was short-lived as others, just like him, simply took his place. Violence continued, and public executions appeared to do very little to curb it. Ironically, there were anecdotal accounts of pickpockets stealing the wallets of individuals amid the crowds that gathered to watch the public executions.[6]

The purpose of these historical examples is not to debate the morality or effectiveness of capital punishment or other forms of punishments. Rather, it is to underscore the real possibility of overzealousness, ignorance, and corruption in our administration of *justice*.

THE STRUGGLE IS REAL

As the wheat is growing into maturity, the weeds are also growing and competing for resources and spreading pests and diseases. The Lord wants us to grow, but the weeds inhibit our growth. A showdown is inevitable. Presuming that enemies will not attack you because you won't attack them is as naïve as thinking a man-eating carnivore will not prey on you simply because you are a vegan.

The presence of the weeds is the more reason the wheat must take its growth seriously. Without the threats and challenges from the weeds, the wheat may become complacent, weak, and careless. The world is a battlefield, not a playground. Therefore, the servant of the Lord must be trained in warfare. God expects all His saints to be in a constant state of preparedness for spiritual battles. He ensured combat readiness of young Israelites who had not been involved in the Canaan conquest wars by allowing some hostile nations to remain in the Promised Land (Judg. 3:1).

If we do not exercise ourselves, our spiritual muscles will atrophy. The weeds keep us on our toes and remind us that, if we are to survive and thrive, slothfulness is not an option.

We must understand that the battle we are fighting is first and foremost spiritual in nature. No amount of political activism, social justice, punitive justice, or policies will transform the hearts of men without the power of the Holy Spirit. And even with the help of the Holy Spirit, evil will not be eradicated in the world until Christ's second coming.

The primary work of the Holy Spirit in the current age is spiritual transformation, not political revolution. Undoubtedly, transformed believers possess the potential to significantly transform the governance of their nations; however, this transformative process commences at the level of the individual heart. Nonetheless, we must not use the anticipation of eschatological judgment as a pretext for unbridled injustice in the here and now.

> *Presuming that enemies will not attack you because you won't attack them is as naïve as thinking a man-eating carnivore will not prey on you simply because you are a vegan.*

Discouraging suffering victims from seeking justice by assuring them they will receive it in heaven is not a helpful response. Rather, we should use our God-given influence to ensure justice is done, but we must acknowledge that this will not always be the case. While we may not be able to light up the entire universe, each of us can brighten the little corner where God has planted us.

Whatever justice is denied here on earth will be attained in heaven. During the Harvest, God will righteously revisit and judge every human interaction, regardless of how we judge them in this world.

Given that our current world is not our final home, any solution we offer humanity must include the everlasting remedy: salvation through Jesus Christ. Lazarus was resurrected by Jesus, and although he probably enjoyed an extended life afterwards, he eventually succumbed to death again. He's been dead for about 2,000 years now. What if his soul was not saved? In the grand scheme of things, what is the significance of being resurrected from the dead, only to live a few more years and ultimately spend eternity in hell?

View your activism as a short-term solution. Remember to also offer the everlasting solution of salvation in Jesus, and in Him alone. It's important to stand up for worthy causes, but we must acknowledge that completely eliminating evil is unrealistic. Yet we will hold the fort until the Master returns. Having this understanding will keep us from feeling frustrated. Maranatha!

THE NURSERY AT HOME

We must understand the significance of the fact that the next generations of wheat and weed are currently being bred in households across the world. In your home, you are either raising wheat or weed. Take a moment to let that sink in.

Future rapists, murderers, prostitutes, fraudsters, cheats, liars, fornicators, and adulterers are being raised, probably inadvertently, as children and teenagers in many homes now. Likewise, future evangelists, pastors, preachers, teachers of the Word, prophets, and godly Christian men and women are being raised in many homes. The two worlds are bound to collide, and this collision may start as early as in elementary school. Therefore, ensure that your wheat is fortified with God's strength and truth to successfully overcome the damaging influence of weeds.

As we nurture the next generation, let us approach our responsibility with utmost seriousness. To flourish, the wheat requires a careful combination of nutrients, water, and attentive care. In contrast, anything goes for the weeds. It's a broad way for them. Consequently, the wheat cannot thrive by adopting the lifestyle of the weeds. Their needs and purposes are different. As the popular saying goes, *others may, but I cannot*. The weed can do as it pleases and still thrive, but the wheat cannot. It's crucial that we continue to emphasize this fact to our children.

In fact, one effective way of neutralizing the wheat is to make it imitate the lifestyle of the weed. If it does, it dies. We should not allow or encourage our children to imitate the ways of the world, even if those ways are popular or promoted by celebrities. Let them know celebrities are not their primary role models. The focus of the wheat should be on the farmer, not on the weeds—either to copy their lifestyle or be excessively critical of them. Our job is to keep "looking unto Jesus, the Author and Finisher of our faith" (Heb. 12:2).

TOLERANCE OR NEGLIGENCE?

Now, we've come to the subject of tolerance. "Let both grow together until the harvest" (Matt. 13:30). Can we equate the growing together of the wheat and weeds to tolerance?

Tolerance has become a buzzword in the world today. Most secular organizations tout their tolerance credentials and wear them as a badge of pride, and the churches are not left far behind. In fact, some churches are ahead of the curve. *Live and let's live* is their new motto.

Does Jesus expect His followers to be tolerant? To answer this question, we need to ask further probing questions. First, how do we define *tolerance*? Second, tolerant of what or whom, exactly? It seems the current use of the word *tolerance* is a spectrum covering almost everything. Its amorphous nature and shape-shifting abilities make it difficult to pin down to a specific definition.

For some people, tolerance is about accepting and supporting what others do or believe in. You are not just expected to avoid frowning upon things you disagree with, but also to actively support and promote them. It is a common occurrence that those who emphasize the importance of tolerance often struggle to exhibit tolerance towards opposing perspectives. Consequently, it has become a shouting and gaslighting contest, where the group with the loudest voice molds and redefines the socio-political and cultural landscapes, dictating which viewpoint can legitimately exhibit intolerance towards other perspectives.

> *In your home, you are either raising wheat or weed. Take a moment to let that sink in.*

This view of tolerance is not congruent with the teachings of the Bible. After cataloguing a litany of sins, Paul said of those committing the sins that

> although they know God's righteous decree that those who do such things deserve death, they not only continue to do these very things but also approve of those who practice them. (Rom. 1:32 NIV)

God not only calls us to abstain from sin and perspectives that contradict His Word, but He also does not expect us to approve of or condone the actions of those who practice such behaviours, even if we ourselves do not engage in them. Tolerance doesn't mean to blend in so much with the world that we become indistinguishable from it. The wheat must resist the temptation to imitate or obsequiously please the weeds. The Bible says,

Therefore, come out from among unbelievers, and separate yourselves from them, says the LORD. Don't touch their filthy things, and I will welcome you. (2 Cor. 6:17 NLT)

Tolerance, as understood from the Biblical perspective, is to show patience and forbearance towards people with whom we disagree. To "gently instruct those who oppose the truth. Perhaps God will change those people's hearts, and they will learn the truth" (2 Tim. 2:25 NLT). Biblical tolerance is "to speak evil of no one, to avoid quarreling, to be gentle, and to show perfect courtesy toward all people" (Titus 3:2 ESV).

The prevailing idea of tolerance assumes that all opinions are equally valid and deserving of respect and celebration. This assumption is not logically coherent, as we all live in communities guided and guarded by laws. The existence of laws implies differences in values and perceptions of actions. Laws imply some actions are legal, while others are *verboten*. By extension, we can argue that not all actions or ideas are equally valid.

In fact, one effective way of neutralizing the wheat is to make it imitate the lifestyle of the weed. If it does, it dies.

Okay, but what if no one is hurt? This is another big trap into which many people often fall, even believers. What such people fail to understand is that any perceived equilibrium between the wheat and weeds is dynamic, not static. The system is in a constant state of competition. Though things may appear calm on the surface, there is always a powerful undercurrent that may bear little semblance to the façade of calmness on the surface. As either the weed or wheat yields ground, the other fills the void. Indeed, nature abhors a vacuum.

The church might believe that while certain ideas are sinful, they do not cause harm to others. Yet experience and recorded history show that often those same ideas grow and come back to haunt the church. The nascent idea that was initially yearning for acceptance, just to live quietly alongside other ideas, soon grows strong and tries to override every other idea, even the ones that once accommodated it in its infancy.

Evil and good can never co-exist peacefully for long. Any perceived peaceful co-existence is merely a ruse to allow one of them to grow strong enough to uproot the other.

For the flesh lusts against the Spirit, and the Spirit against the flesh; and these are contrary to one another, so that you do not do the things that you wish. (Gal. 5:17)

Although we wrestle not against flesh and blood (humans), we wrestle, nonetheless. It is not the duty of believers to actively seek out and target individuals whose lifestyle they find objectionable. Never forget that the devil is the real enemy. You cannot defeat the devil by destroying a fellow human. By first defeating the devil in the spiritual realm, his ideas in the physical realm gradually lose their power.

Tolerance is a Christian virtue. It allows us to boldly proclaim our faith while treating those who oppose us with gentleness and respect. God shows us the perfect example of tolerance: "For He gives His sunlight to both the evil and the good, and He sends rain on the just and the unjust alike" (Matt. 5:45 NLT). But along with His generous blessings, He keeps sending preachers to call the unjust to repentance. Thus, Biblical tolerance and speaking the truth in love are not mutually exclusive.

Smiling and joking with a man walking on a rail track while a train is fast approaching is not love or tolerance. It is pure wickedness. It is *hate speech*. True love alerts him to the impending danger. Pushing him out of harm's way if need be is probably a great idea too.

Jesus showed us the perfect balance of tolerance and truth when He told the woman caught in adultery, "Neither do I condemn you; go and sin no more" (John 8:11). Both parts of the statement carry equal weight. Unfortunately, some choose to cherry-pick either the *Neither do I condemn you* part (tolerance and forgiveness) or the *Go and sin no more* part (holiness).

SAME FIELD; DIFFERENT DESTINIES

"Then I will tell the harvesters to sort out the weeds, tie them into bundles, and burn them, and to put the wheat in the barn" (vv. 28–30). The wheat and the weed have distinctly different futures awaiting them. They may be intertwined here on earth, but they will be separated in the afterlife.

A man and his wife may be intertwined on earth but may not share the same eternal destiny. As the inspired Psalmist said, the godly and the ungodly will be separated in eternity. "Therefore, the ungodly shall not stand in the judgment, nor sinners in the congregation of the righteous" (Psa. 1:5). The wheat will be gathered into the barn, unto the Father in heaven, while the weeds will be bundled and burned.

In a sense, only two judgment days for sin are available to every human: one in the past and one in the future. The former event took place at the Cross of Calvary in the past, whereas the latter event will happen at the Great White Throne in the future. By choosing the Cross, we can avoid the wrath of the Great White Throne Judgment, as our sins would have been judged and forgiven.

> *It is a common occurrence that those who emphasize the importance of tolerance struggle to exhibit tolerance towards opposing perspectives.*

The Cross has fully satisfied God's anger towards our sins. For the believers, *it is indeed finished!* Fully paid. Jesus has paid it all! Our judgment day of sin was at the Cross of Calvary. Therefore, we are not afraid of the Great White Throne Judgment. *Rock of Ages, cleft for me. Let me hide myself in Thee!*

Those who reject Christ's finished work of atonement on the Cross will directly face the wrath of God at the sombre Great White Throne Judgment. God will judge unbelievers from every era for their sins and rejection of the truth revealed to them during their lifetimes. They will all be sent to the lake of fire. This judgment will occur after the millennial reign of Christ (Rev. 20:7–10). In the book of Revelation, the Great White Throne Judgment is depicted as follows:

> Then I saw a great white throne and Him who sat on it, from whose face the earth and the heaven fled away. And there was found no place for them. And I saw the dead, small and great, standing before God, and books were opened. And another book was opened, which is the Book of Life. And the dead were judged according to their works, by the things which were written in the books. The sea gave up the dead who were in it, and Death and Hades delivered up the dead who were in them. And they were judged, each one according to his works. Then Death and Hades were cast into the lake of fire. This is the second death. And anyone not found written in the Book of Life was cast into the lake of fire. (Rev. 20:11–15 NKJV)

In contradistinction to the gloomy fate of the weeds, the wheat will face the Judgment Seat of Christ, where the quality of their service to God, rather than their sins, will be judged. Apostle Paul described it thus:

> For we must all appear before the judgment seat of Christ, that each one may receive the things done in the body, according to what we have done whether good or bad. (2 Cor. 5:10)

During the ancient Olympics games, a judge would sit on a seat called the *Bema* to determine which athletes in the race came in first, second, and so on. He would also give rewards or prizes to the winners based on his judgment of their performances. In the Christian tradition, the Judgment Seat of Christ is also referred to as the *Bema*, drawing a parallel to the ancient Olympics games. Christ observes how believers run their race and interact with one another. He determines who is disqualified, the order of performances, and the appropriate rewards.

> *Smiling and joking with a man walking along a rail track while a train is fast approaching is not love or tolerance ... True love alerts him to the impending danger.*

Believers labour in God's vineyard here on earth, but Christ remains the ultimate judge of our works. The quality of every believer's work will be tested by passing it through the fire; that is, every work will be scrutinized under Christ's holy gaze and according to His standard. Some works, made of wood, hay, and stubble, will burn under His intense gaze.

The owners of such works would have laboured in vain, as their works would be disqualified and thus not rewarded in heaven. This could be due to working with wrong motives and motivations or failing to adhere to God's pattern and instructions. In essence, such believers have been busy doing nothing. They will count themselves blessed to have even made it to heaven at all—safe in heaven but *smell like fire* under the intense gaze of Christ. Paul said it like this: "If anyone's work is burned up, he will suffer loss, though he himself will be saved, but only as through fire" (1 Cor. 3:15 ESV).

Some believers will receive great rewards because of the quality and purity of their works. When they fed the poor, they didn't do it to be seen or celebrated. In fact, many of them didn't have thoughts of being rewarded in heaven while they were helping the needy. Their works were made of silver and gold.

> Then the righteous will answer him, "Lord, when did we see you hungry and feed you, or thirsty and give you something to drink?" ... The King will reply, "Truly I tell you, whatever you did for one of the least of these brothers and sisters of mine, you did for me." (Matt. 25:37,40 NIV)

IN THE MEANTIME

In the meantime, we should entrust judgment to God and focus on our spiritual growth and spreading the gospel. Jesus asked us to grow, and grow we must. He also said, "Occupy till I come" (Luke 19:13 KJV). Therefore, we must stay engaged and stand our ground. Each position held by the wheat is one less position available to the weeds.

Our judgment day of sin was at the Cross of Calvary. Therefore, we are not afraid of the Great White Throne Judgment.

Don't run or hide from the world; instead, thrive in it. There is no perfect place in the world, not even the Vatican City or Jerusalem. So, thrive where God has planted you. Be firm in your faith and boldly declare it, but do not attack or destroy those with contrary opinions.

The Farmer is confident that the wheat has what it takes to compete with and triumph over the weed. As long as it doesn't become unequally yoked with the weed, it will not succumb to pest infestation, disease, or death. It will not be taken away from the world prematurely, but divine Providence will keep it from the hand of the evil one. Observe Jesus' prayer for the wheat: "My prayer is not that you [God] take them out of the world but that you protect them from the evil one" (John 17:15 NIV).

As we hold the fort, let us continue to anticipate and prepare for the Harvest. Will you be bundled with the wheat or the weeds during the Harvest? Our heartfelt cry should be: "Gather not my soul with sinners, nor my life with bloody men" (Psa. 26:9 KJV) but let me "be bound in the bundle of the living with the LORD [my] God" (1 Sam. 25:29).

Yet we should note that "where the tree falls, there it shall lie" (Eccles. 11:3). If we huddle with the weeds now, we can expect to be bundled with them at the Harvest. The rule is: *huddle now, bundle then.*

The wheat will be gathered unto God in heaven, from the first wheat (Abel) who was cut down in his prime by the weed (Cain) to the last saint of God to ever tread this earth. All will be gathered unto Him in heaven, including all our saved loved ones who have departed the world at various times through the ages. God's desire to reunite with His saints is captured in Psalm 50 where He said, "Gather My saints together to Me, those who have made a covenant with Me by sacrifice" (Psa. 50:5).

> *The quality of every believer's work will be tested by passing it through the fire; that is, every work will be scrutinized under Christ's holy gaze and according to His standard.*

Secure with their Lord and Saviour, there will be no more sun to scorch them, no more weeds to afflict them, and no Satan to beguile or slander them. Finally, they will forever be safe in the hollow of His hand.

When You come to collect Your people, remember me, Oh Lord, my God!

Chapter 9

The Yeast

Jesus also used this illustration: "The Kingdom of Heaven is like the yeast a woman used in making bread. Even though she put only a little yeast in three measures of flour, it permeated every part of the dough."

MATTHEW 13:33 (NLT)

Yeast primarily functions as a leavening agent, initiating the fermentation process that makes dough rise. It improves the texture and taste of bread, while also strengthening the dough. If yeast is not used, bread will lack the light and fluffy texture it typically has. When flour is mixed with water in the presence of yeast, all the ingredients necessary for fermentation are present. The dough rises as a result of the carbon dioxide released by the yeast present in it. In a sense, the dough is *alive*, teeming with microbes before it is baked in the oven.

The yeast mentioned in this parable is not the typical cute packets of yeast we are familiar with. It is more like a sourdough starter, which is made from the fermentation of a mixture of fresh flour and water. Once the ingredients are combined, the culture starts to undergo fermentation and encourages the growth of the natural yeasts present in the environment. To leaven future dough mixes, a small portion of the sourdough starter is added as a leavening agent. For a quicker and more efficient process, the baker can decide to reserve a portion of the dough from one batch and use it as a leavening agent for the next.

The exact timeline of when humans started using yeasts and other microbes for bread baking is unclear. It was probably discovered by accident at some point in ancient history. Someone probably left a mixed dough sitting out on a warm day, only to return and find that the dough has risen. Fermentation had occurred—unplanned.

YEAST IN THE BIBLE

There are several references to yeast in the Bible. The first significant entry of yeast into the spiritual consciousness of the Israelites was when God liberated them from their slavery in Egypt. They had to move quickly, and in their haste, they baked and ate unleavened bread with the dough they brought out of Egypt (Exo. 12:39).

In commemoration of this significant event, God instructed them to celebrate a week of feasting called the Feast of Unleavened Bread starting on the day after the Passover Day (Lev. 23:4–6). During this week of feasting, they must remove all yeast from their houses and mustn't eat any bread that contained yeast (Exo. 12:15; 13:6–7).

The Bible often portrays yeast in a bad light. In Biblical symbolism, fermentation implies corruption, which represents sin, evil, hypocrisy, and the spread of corrupt beliefs and influences. Jesus referred to the evil doctrine of the Pharisees and Sadducees as *the yeast of the Pharisees and Sadducees* (Matt. 16:6–12). He also referred to the propaganda (equivalent to today's media influence) of King Herod as *the yeast of Herod* (Mark 8:15–21). Further, Paul used yeast as a symbol of the corrupting influence of sin among the Corinthian and Galatian churches (1 Cor. 5:6–8; Gal. 5:9).

Considering the Biblical references above, some individuals believe that the parable of the yeast further reinforces the negative portrayal of yeast in the Bible. They argue that Jesus used this parable to alert us to the subtle infiltration of false doctrines within the church, which could potentially corrupt the essence of the gospel. However, there is no such trace of negativity or evidence to support it in this concise parable.

On the contrary, Jesus used this parable to highlight the positive working of God's kingdom, from its small beginning to the glorious impact it would eventually have on the entire world. This is consistent with the other parables that Jesus used to describe the kingdom of God. For example, in the parable of the mustard seed, the seed started small but grew into a mighty tree. Similarly, the gospel started small in Jerusalem, but it did not end there. It worked its way to all Judea, then Samaria, and finally to the ends of the earth (Acts 1:8). It worked its way through three measures of flour.

It is in this positive light that Jesus used yeast in this parable. This parable shows that yeast can sometimes connote positivity. After all, just because evil can work its way through good does not mean good cannot work its way through evil.

THE KINGDOM OF GOD IS SEEDED FROM THE OUTSIDE

The first lesson from this parable is that the kingdom of God is seeded from the outside. As the dough cannot leaven itself, humanity cannot save itself. Salvation must come from an external source. Corrupt humanity does not have the agency to redeem itself. Help and redemption must come from a source outside of our nature. In his epistle to the Romans, Paul aptly portrayed the utter helplessness of our corrupt human nature thus:

> For I know that in me (that is, in my flesh) nothing good dwells; for to will is present with me, but how to perform what is good I do not find. (Rom. 7:18)

Willpower can do some good, but it has its limits. We cannot *will* ourselves into salvation or transformation. We need the quickening Spirit of God to transform us from death to life. "It is the Spirit who gives life; the flesh profits nothing. The words that I speak to you are spirit, and they are life" (John 6:63).

Salvation is not the beautification of the spiritually dead to make them look presentable. It is the resurrection of the spiritually dead to life in Christ. It is so power-intensive that it can only be accomplished by the same power that raised Jesus from the dead. Salvation cannot be achieved through human effort; it is simply a miracle.

You cannot save your unbelieving children by simply having a heart-to-heart talk with them. They are dead spiritually and dead people do not respond to talks. Threats may make them put up a front to appease you, but don't forget that "the wrath of man does not produce the righteousness of God" (James 1:20).

The only thing a dead person responds to is the quickening resurrection power that can bring it back to life. Sure, we may have the *talk* with people, but we must understand what is going on behind the scenes. If our words are not backed up by the power of the Holy Spirit, we might as well be speaking to a corpse. Since there is no life in the corpse, life must be infused into it from the outside.

THE KINGDOM OF GOD GROWS WITHIN

The second lesson is that the kingdom of God is within us. Although it is seeded from the outside, its growth occurs internally. Its working within us is what brings victory over sin and its attendant consequences. The Psalmist said, "Your word I have hidden in my heart, That I might not sin against You" (Psa. 119:11).

Yeast makes dough rise from within. The influence of God's kingdom begins with the inner man. The foundational change that God brings about is in the individual's heart, and this internal change soon becomes apparent through external manifestations. Just as water cleanses the inside of a cup before overflowing to cleanse the outside (Matt. 23:26), the grace we've received must first save us before it can save others through our testimony. Grace must deal with sin *in* us before it can deal with sin *around* us.

> The Bible often portrays yeast in a bad light. In Biblical symbolism, fermentation implies corruption, which represents sin, evil, hypocrisy, and the spread of corrupt beliefs and influences.

Christians living in ungodly cultures do not work from the outside in; they work from the inside out. They serve as agents of change even without holding positions of secular power. They understand the limits of government policies and regulations. Moreover, they understand that the world is not going to be saved by externally imposed rules.

Policies and laws may constrain outward appearances and behaviours, but only the gospel can transform a person into a new creation. Only grace can turn the vilest sinner into the holiest saint.

There was a time in Jesus' life when the people wanted to crown Him as their king. A lot of people would have gladly accepted that offer or even fought for it, but Jesus declined the offer. John reported the incident as follows:

> Therefore, when Jesus perceived that they were about to come and take Him by force to make Him king, He departed again to the mountain by Himself alone. (John 6:15)

Why did Jesus reject the offer of kingship? Wouldn't that have provided him with the necessary platform and visibility to connect with a larger audience, while also granting him the political clout to bring about meaningful change? Let us be wary of bringing carnal thinking into kingdom business. Listen to Jesus' response to the people:

> My kingdom is not of this world. If it were, My servants would fight to prevent My arrest by the Jewish leaders. But now My kingdom is from another place. (John 18:36)

Jesus wanted a kingdom that works its way from the inside out. His disciples didn't understand Him at first, and they must have felt frustrated by His *failure* to make the most of His opportunities. Peter, the *self-appointed lord-in-waiting*, even flexed his muscles by slicing off the ear of Malchus, a servant of the high priest (John 18:10–11).

Just as Moses tried to liberate the enslaved Israelites by his own might (Exo. 2:11–12), Peter wanted to save Jesus by his own physical strength. How feasible was that though? Could Moses have withstood the mighty army of Pharaoh all by himself? Could Peter have single-handedly stopped the Jews and the Romans from capturing Jesus?

> *You cannot save your unbelieving children by simply having a heart-to-heart talk with them. They are dead spiritually and dead people do not respond to talks.*

These two men, though lived millennia apart, soon learned that "by strength shall no man prevail" (1 Sam. 2:9). The victory will be won but "not by might nor by power, but by My Spirit, says the LORD of hosts" (Zech. 4:6).

Many believers are eager to see God's kingdom come upon the earth, and they want His will to be done here as it is in heaven. The problem is: They do not want it to begin with them. It's nothing short of mere virtue signalling to expect God to fix the world when we haven't allowed Him to fix us. Salvation is not about the theatrics or melodrama of signs in the sky. The kingdom of God does not come with observation (Luke 17:20–21). The grace that hasn't transformed your life cannot save your soul or those of others.

THE KINGDOM OF GOD HAS SMALL BEGINNINGS

The third lesson from this parable is that the kingdom of God has small beginnings. Who would have thought that salvation would come out of Nazareth!

The Saviour of the world did not cruise down from heaven in a grand procession of cherubim in chariots of fire surrounded by legions of angels. Instead, He arrived as a tiny baby, born in a humble stable in the small town of Bethlehem to a struggling family, who could only afford to present a pair of turtledoves, a customary offering for the poor, for His dedication at the Temple (Luke 2:24; Lev. 12:8).

To make matters worse—or better—the Messiah did not come from any of the respectable towns in Judea. He came from Galilee—the *Galilee of the Gentiles* (Isa. 9:1; Matt. 4:13–16). He probably had a distinctive Galilean Aramaic accent, which would have been easily recognized by the Judeans. The accent of Peter, a fellow Galilean (from Bethsaida), gave him away during Jesus' trial (Matt. 26:73). Even Nathanael, who was a despised Galilean himself (John 21:2), looked down on *this Galilean* from Nazareth, and asked, "Can

> *Policies and laws may constrain outward appearances and behaviours, but only the gospel can transform a person into a new creation.*

anything good come out of Nazareth?" (John 1:46). Thus, addressing a Galilean Nazarene as the Messiah would have been taken as a sort of joke at first. Indeed, Jesus came as the reject of the rejects.

The primary carriers of the gospel were not twelve noblemen or elites. Jesus gave the responsibility of spreading the gospel to twelve ordinary men, probably unsophisticated men with limited education. As unbelievable as it may sound, the entire world was set on fire by the words of these men.

Throughout history, the kingdom of God often appeared weak compared to the mighty human empires within which it existed. This statement holds true even to this day. In various countries across the globe, believers who hold true to their faith face constant persecution, albeit to varying degrees. In most instances, they are in the minority and have little political or economic power. Yet the more persecuted they are, the more resilient they become. They thrive in the midst of their formidable adversaries.

God often gives us great visions in embryonic forms. If we get discouraged by the insignificant size of what we have in our hand, we may never see it grow into what we have in our heart. Great things often start small. If we do not give up, we will see our visions grow. When the vision finally becomes a reality, not only do we get to fully enjoy its beauty, but in the process, we would have learned how to nurture nascent visions to maturity.

THE KINGDOM OF GOD GROWS AGAINST ALL ODDS

The fourth lesson from this parable is that the kingdom of God grows, against all odds. Though it begins small, it does not remain small. It will grow as guaranteed by the Almighty God Himself. Therefore, let us "not despise these small beginnings, for the LORD rejoices to see the work begin, to see the plumb line in Zerubbabel's hand" (Zech. 4:10). God rejoices over small beginnings—because He can see the great endings—and so should we.

Relatively speaking, the yeast was small, yet it worked its way through the dough. Similarly, the gospel looked weak in the face of the pervasive idol worship in Ephesus. Yet the Word grew so mightily through the dough of the ungodly Ephesian culture until it prevailed and turned Ephesian sinners into saints (Acts 19:20).

The gospel can be likened to a lion. It doesn't need our help to be a predator; it only needs to be let loose to do its job. Rather than spend our time contemplating whether the gospel can change lives, why not simply let it loose? Just preach it, and let God handle the rest.

> *Throughout history, the kingdom of God often appeared weak compared to the mighty human empires within which it existed.*

We often underestimate the inherent transformative power of the gospel. The Word sown into the life of the vilest sinner may appear too weak to have any effect. Yet one is often pleasantly surprised to see the simple words of the gospel bring hardened sinners to their knees in tearful repentance.

Many powerful rulers and influential individuals bragged about how easily they would eradicate Christianity. And try, they did. But they failed. Ironically, while their mighty empires are long gone and their influences have waned, the *weak* kingdom of God is still here and thriving. Hallelujah!

> And from the time John the Baptist began preaching until now, the kingdom of Heaven has been forcefully advancing, and violent people are attacking it. (Matt. 11:12 NLT)

Many Caesars tried to stamp out Christianity by killing its adherents. Regardless, it prevailed against the might of Rome. The infamous list of the enemies of the Cross includes Emperors Nero (started a blanket persecution of Christians), Vespasian (demolished the Jerusalem Temple in AD 70), Domitian (exiled Apostle John to the isle of Patmos), Diocletian (of the *Diocletianic* or *Great Persecution*), Trajan, Decius (of the *Decian Persecution*), and Valerian.

In AD 303, Emperor Diocletian, an avowed enemy of the Cross, ordered a direct attack on Christians. He wanted Christianity eradicated once and for all on February 23, the feast of the Terminalia, the Roman god of boundaries. His soldiers burned down the newly built church in Nicomedia (in what is now Turkey), executed the Christians found in the city, and burned all the copies of the Bible they could find.[1-3]

Seventeen centuries later, Diocletian, his empire, and his armies are long gone, while the kingdom of God endures and flourishes. But it did not take 1700 years for the gospel to prevail over Diocletian. The emperor stepped down in AD 305,[4] probably due to ill-health. In AD 312, just nine years after his deadly decree, one of his successors, Constantine I, led his army to the Battle of Milvian Bridge with the Christian cross placed on their shields![5] Emperor Theodosius I made Nicene Christianity the official state religion of the Roman Empire with the Edict of Thessalonica in AD 380, a mere 77 years after Diocletian's decree.[6]

THE KINGDOM IS QUICK AND QUICKENING

The fifth lesson from the parable is that the kingdom of God is quick and quickening. Like the yeast, the Word of God *is* alive and *makes* alive. At first, the microbes are limited to the sourdough, but they rapidly multiply, eventually transforming the entire dough into a bustling ecosystem of microbes. The kingdom of God works in a similar way.

> For the word of God is quick, and powerful, and sharper than any two-edged sword, piercing even to the dividing asunder of soul and spirit, and of the joints and marrow, and is a discerner of the thoughts and intents of the heart. (Heb. 4:12)

The Word brought Lazarus out of his grave, and it can bring you out of yours as well. It can inject vitality into every dead area of your life. No rot is too hopeless for the Word to reinvigorate with life. It can make testimonies out of your hopeless situations.

The gospel can be likened to a lion. It doesn't need our help to be a predator; it only needs to be let loose to do it job.

The Word is very active. Like yeast, it spreads quickly beyond its point of origin. Although it works silently, its effect soon becomes clear to all. Such is the work of grace in our hearts. It works as silent as light; yet it warms and illuminates the crevices of the human soul. It spreads throughout the world, reaching even the seemingly inaccessible places, until its impact is felt everywhere.

God's kingdom is not bound up in one place like a lump of clay. Just like salt in a broth, the less lumpy and the more diffuse it is, the better its effect. The kingdom doesn't have to be spectacular, flashy, or impressive to grow. The Holy Spirit—working through means often despised by the world as being weak and foolish—keeps changing the world, one soul at a time.

> But we preach Christ crucified: a stumbling block to Jews and foolishness to Gentiles, but to those whom God has called, both Jews and Greeks, Christ the power of God and the wisdom of God. For the foolishness of God is wiser than human wisdom, and the weakness of God is stronger than human strength. (1 Cor. 1:23–25 NIV)

THE EFFECT OF GOD'S KINGDOM IS COMPREHENSIVE

The sixth lesson from this parable is that the effect of the kingdom of God is comprehensive. Only a little yeast is kneaded into the dough, yet given enough time, it spreads through the entire dough.

The *measure* (or *cor*) is an ancient unit of measurement for both liquids and dry materials, as stated in 1 Kings 5:11. Determining the exact modern equivalent weight for the three measures of flour mentioned in the parable is challenging due to conflicting estimates from various sources. However, it is reasonable to assume that it was a significant quantity, possibly several kilogrammes, enough to bake a considerable quantity of bread.

For comparison, the extravagant King Solomon's daily ration for his palace was thirty measures of fine flour (1 Kings 4:22)—just ten times what the woman was baking. This suggests that the woman was probably not baking solely for her own household. She was baking to feed many people. This hints at a major attribute of God's kingdom: It is not a self-serving enterprise. It reaches and serves all the nations of the world.

Jesus is in effect saying that even a little yeast is enough to affect a large quantity of dough. The Word, hidden in the human heart, can transform the spirit, soul, and body—all three measures.

A little light bulb is enough to illuminate a large room full of darkness. The little *you* can make a significant difference wherever God has planted you. Never underestimate yourself! A pinch of salt can make all the difference to a large broth of soup. Rather than being intimidated by the sheer size of the challenge ahead of you, focus on the One inside of you. For "He who is in you is greater than he who is in the world" (1 John 4:4).

> *The stone that killed Goliath was not as big as his head. You don't need to be larger than life to have larger-than-life impacts.*

The stone that killed Goliath was not as big as his head. You don't need to be larger than life to have larger-than-life impacts. What matters is the power that is backing you. Viewed through the lens of faith, the big intimidating challenge becomes a target too big to miss.

The gospel might have originated in an obscure part of the world, but today the earth is being filled with the knowledge of the glory of the LORD, as the waters cover the sea (Hab. 2:14).

Chapter 10

THE SHREWD MANAGER

❧❧❧❧❧❧❧❧❧❧

Jesus told this story to his disciples: "There was a certain rich man who had a manager handling his affairs. One day a report came that the manager was wasting his employer's money. So the employer called him in and said, 'What's this I hear about you? Get your report in order, because you are going to be fired.' The manager thought to himself, 'Now what? My boss has fired me. I don't have the strength to dig ditches, and I'm too proud to beg. Ah, I know how to ensure that I'll have plenty of friends who will give me a home when I am fired.' So he invited each person who owed money to his employer to come and discuss the situation. He asked the first one, 'How much do you owe him?' The man replied, 'I owe him 800 gallons of olive oil.' So, the manager told him, 'Take the bill and quickly change it to 400 gallons.' 'And how much do you owe my employer?' he asked the next man. 'I owe him 1,000 bushels of wheat,' was the reply. 'Here,' the manager said, 'take the bill and change it to 800 bushels.'

The rich man had to admire the dishonest rascal for being so shrewd. And it is true that the children of this world are more shrewd in dealing with the world around them than are the children of the light. Here's the lesson: Use your worldly resources to benefit others and make friends. Then, when your possessions are gone, they will welcome you to an eternal home. If you are faithful in little things, you will be faithful in large ones. But if you are dishonest in little things, you won't be honest with greater responsibilities. And if you are untrustworthy about worldly wealth, who will trust you with

the true riches of heaven? And if you are not faithful with other people's things, why should you be trusted with things of your own?

LUKE 16:1–12 (NLT)

People have hurled several epithets at the steward in this parable; for example, he's been called the unrighteous, dishonest, unjust, mischievous, unscrupulous, or shrewd steward. The interpretations offered for the parable are as numerous as, if not more than, the epithets. Though Jesus gave a clear interpretation of the parable, many people still struggle with it because of their *a priori* assumption that God or Jesus must be the protagonist in all of Jesus' parables. For example, in the parable of the prodigal son, the father represents God. Similarly, in the parable of the wedding banquet, the king represents God. But in this parable, the protagonist was an unscrupulous manager. Understandably, many people are at a loss to know who represents God or Jesus in this parable.

We can easily clear up this confusion by admitting there are no rules specifying that God or Jesus must be the protagonist of any or all of Jesus' parables. He told us these parables to teach us deep spiritual lessons, and we shouldn't get fixated on some expectations of who or what the main characters in the parables must be. What is important is for us to consider the context in which Jesus told each parable, rather than imposing our personal biases on it.

It is possible to learn something good from people who may not be of the best character or reputation. If we can learn from animals and inanimate objects, maybe we can also learn one or two things from a human, made in God's image and likeness, even if the image has been deformed. King Solomon said, "Go to the ant, you sluggard; consider its ways and be wise!" (Prov. 6:6 NLT). If the *human* sluggard can learn from the ant, humans can learn from one another.

Soldiers sometimes, and maybe often, admire the courage of their adversaries on the battlefield. Even though they may not agree with the adversary's cause and goals, they admire the courage with which they pursue their *misguided* cause. Similarly, politicians across political divides may not see eye to eye, but they may admire the unity and political sagacity displayed by their opponents.

It is sometimes a case of honour among thieves. Even criminals may have a code of conduct to enforce discipline and trust among themselves. For example, criminals may have a code preventing them from stealing from one another or taking each other's spouses. Thus, the police unit that abandons its wounded personnel to bleed out and die may learn a thing or two from the armed robbers who make sure none of their comrades are left behind. That does not equate to condoning armed robbery; it simply means one can learn something good even from the most unpleasant people or experiences. Such is the case with this parable.

THE CONTRAST-AND-DEGREE METHOD

Jesus often used what I would term the *contrast-and-degree* method to drive home His point. He would highlight some good attribute found in otherwise evil people, and would, in a manner of speaking, rhetorically ask His audience: "If evil people can do something good for their loved ones, can you imagine how much good the good God would do for His own children?" In some instances, He would challenge His audience to do better than the evil people.

This method does not endorse the totality of the actions of the evil people; it only pinpoints their good attributes, either to challenge us to have more faith in God's ability and desire to take care of us or as a reminder that God expects us to do better than the evil people.

Though we can find several examples of the *contrast-and-degree* method in the Scripture, two examples from the book of Matthew are presented below:

> Which of you, if your son asks for bread, will give him a stone? Or if he asks for a fish, will give him a snake? If you, then, though you are evil, know how to give good gifts to your children, how much more will your Father in heaven give good gifts to those who ask Him! (Matt. 7:9–11 NIV)

> If you love only those who love you, what reward is there for that? Even corrupt tax collectors do that much. (Matt. 5:46 NLT)

The good attribute Jesus highlighted in the example He gave in Matthew 7:9–11 is that even perverse people give good gifts to their children. The lesson is: If evil people still care for the needs of their children, how much more would the quintessentially good God provide for the needs of His own children? Obviously, God is not equating Himself with evil people. He is simply strengthening our faith in His ability and willingness to take care of our needs.

> *If we can learn from animals and inanimate objects, maybe we can also learn one or two things from a human, made in God's image and likeness, even if the image has been deformed.*

For this parable, our goal should be to identify the good attributes Jesus is highlighting in the shrewd manager, and to ask ourselves how we can develop these attributes to a greater and purer extent. We shouldn't become so fixated on minute details that we end up missing the forest for the trees.

CRUXES OF THE MATTER

Though the first verse of the chapter (Luke 16) identifies the primary audience as Jesus' disciples, further in the passage, we get to understand there was a secondary audience, which included some Pharisees. "The Pharisees, who loved money, heard all this and were sneering at Jesus" (Luke 16:14 NIV).

The Pharisees understood the parable was about the love of money. Jesus didn't correct their understanding of the parable, probably indicating they got it right. Even a broken clock is right twice a day. What He corrected was their hypocrisy and the rotten conditions of their hearts:

> Then He said to them, "You like to appear righteous in public, but God knows your hearts. What this world honours is detestable in the sight of God." (Luke 16:15 NLT)

Thus, we can infer that somewhere in the parable lies a warning about the love of money, hypocrisy, and the contrast between God's value system and that of the world. It is with this understanding that we approach this parable.

In this parable, a rich man called his steward to render an account of his financial management. The accusation that triggered this audit was prodigality—the steward had been accused of wasting his master's money. Apparently, the master believed the accusation and threatened to fire his manager, but not before he rendered his account.

The manager got the message and understood he was, for all intents and purposes, already fired. Though his master said he was *going to be fired*, he assumed he *was already fired*. He didn't take any chances or entertain any hope of not being fired. He became proactive and started planning for life after his dismissal.

What could he do to survive and take care of his needs? Dig ditches for pay? No, he was a fat cat too soft for a hard life. What about begging alms or money from friends? Definitely not. He was probably a guy who was highly respected, loved to spend money, and was the life of the party. He could never stoop so low as to beg for favours—he was accustomed to doling them out, not receiving them. "Yes! That's it! *Doling out favours!* That's the trick!" He has finally found his way out.

What if he doles out favours to people in anticipation of them returning the favour when he's finally out of a job? Sounds good—especially if it won't be at his expense. That way, he can get the people in his debt and later approach them for help in a dignified manner. After all, one good turn deserves another.

He began to put his scheme into action by inviting those indebted to his master to gather and discuss their financial obligations. He advised the individual with a debt of 800 gallons of olive oil to alter the amount to 400 gallons on his bill, offering him a 50% discount at the expense of his master. He did the same for the one owing 1000 bushels of wheat. He told him to change it to 800 bushels. They all made the changes on their bills in their own handwritings, not the manager's—he must have really wanted to cover his tracks.

Somehow, the master got to know about his rascally manager's shenanigans. And here comes a major twist in the story: Based on the trends in the other parables, one would expect an immediate and severe judgment on the manager; however, in this case, the master found his manager's shrewdness impressive!

Jesus didn't say anything about the actions the master took to forestall the plans of his manager, or the punishment eventually meted to him. However, we can infer that the manager did not get away with his dishonesty. Jesus left that part out of the story because it wasn't relevant to the point He wanted to make. He has finished with the lesson, and it is important that we set our gaze exactly where Christ wants it.

Applying the *contrast-and-degree* method discussed earlier, we will start by identifying the good attributes of this otherwise dishonest manager.

GOOD SITUATIONAL AWARENESS

The manager had a good understanding of his situation. Although his master was still contemplating his dismissal, he immediately adopted the mindset of someone already fired. "The manager thought to himself, 'Now what? My boss has fired me'" (v. 3). He didn't stick around in the hope that his master would change his mind. From the look of things, he could tell his fate was sealed.

What can we learn from this? The Bible says, "And it is appointed unto men once to die, but after this the judgment" (Heb. 9:27). The appointment to die (for all humans) is like the appointment to be fired (for the manager). However, unlike the manager who understood the irrevocability of his sack and acted as if he was *already fired*, humans do not act as if they are already dead. Acting as if *already dead* in this context means making plans for the inevitable: death.

We dislike being reminded of death. It is one topic we avoid as much as possible, until it eventually strikes. Our approach is often that of crossing the bridge when we get to it. The manager was shrewd in his understanding of the inevitability of his sack, whereas many people, even when just a few seconds away from death, do not want to face the reality of it.

We go through several phases in our lives, and we often make up excuses to avoid facing our mortality in each phase. When young, we are too carefree to think about death. When in middle age, we are too busy to think about it. In old age, we are either too frightened or hardened to think about death. Simply put, throughout our lives, we are either too young, too busy, too frightened, or too hardened—until we are too dead—to think about death.

One of the lessons we can learn from this shrewd manager is to always live with eternity in view. Barring the Rapture of the saints, death is a debt owed by all. So why not live with that consciousness? Not with a morbid fear of death or an unwholesome fascination with it that renders us useless on this side of eternity, but with a clear sense of how precious each minute we have on earth is. May the good Lord "teach us to realize the brevity of life, so that we may grow in wisdom" (Psa. 90:12 NLT).

MAKING PLANS FOR THE INEVITABLE

The manager made plans for the inevitable. His understanding of the finality of his fate wasn't just an academic exercise for him. While it's true that most people dislike discussing death, many philosophers and intellectuals appear to be more embracing of the topic, often with a characteristic stoic courage and curiosity. However, they often treat the topic of death as a purely academic exercise in which they are neutral and objective observers.

They do not appreciate the gravity of the personal implications of the subject. Mortality, judgment, and eternity have graver implications than merely satisfying academic curiosity. They are the most crucial topics to which every human should give careful consideration—while there's still time.

> *Simply put, throughout our lives, we are either too young, too busy, too frightened, or too hardened—until we are too dead—to think about death.*

We often put more thought into college applications and our careers than we give to these weighty matters, even though we may end up not working with the degrees we earn. Whereas college degrees and careers, at best, last only a lifetime, these matters have everlasting implications. Yet we pay very little attention to them.

The dishonest manager displayed more shrewdness than we normally do. He didn't put the issue of his sealed fate on the back burner. Rather, it became the all-consuming passion of his life. He needed to make plans for the inevitable. He considered his options: digging or begging. Once he concluded in his heart that he didn't want to end up as a ditch digger or a beggar, he began to craft the future he wanted for himself: a future of comfort and being welcomed by friends.

Many of us are no strangers to strategic planning. We strategically plan for most aspects of our lives: family, marriage, career, health, and retirement. Our problem seems to be that of priority and value. We typically prioritize what we value, and we tend to forget about things we don't consider important.

For instance, we value money, so we prioritize it. To ensure we have enough of it in retirement, we start making plans right from when we are in our twenties or thirties. If we meet a friend in her forties who seems to give little to no thoughts to her retirement, we chide and remind her that time is running out fast. We encourage her to act responsibly by planning for her future retirement. Yet she may reach death before retirement. Even if she makes it to retirement, it's still a temporary state, whereas death leads to an eternal state.

I remember the story of a king who called his court jester (also known as *the fool*) to his deathbed. Though the king was known for his love of good jokes, he was in no mood for jokes. Terribly ill and terrified of what awaited him on the other side, he had asked all the wise men in his kingdom about his fate, but none could give him a satisfactory answer. In desperation, he turned to the apparent least likely source of wisdom, his court jester, who appeared genuinely surprised by the king's question. The jester whispered to the dying king:

> I have known you for many years as a wise and diligent king. You would make 3-month preparations for 3-day trips so that you would lack nothing in comfort. But here you are, about to make a journey of no return—with zero preparation. And people call me the court fool!

Like the dying king, many of us are good at making detailed plans for ephemeral things yet fail to prepare for our eternal destination.

Where do you see yourself in eternity? Like the manager, consider your options. Do you see yourself in hell for all eternity? Do you picture yourself in the blazing furnace where there will be weeping and gnashing of teeth? (Matt. 13:50). Do you see yourself being "punished with everlasting destruction and shut out from the presence of the Lord and from the glory of his might"? (2 Thess. 1:9 NIV). If these imageries are not the eternal future you desire for yourself, then make plans to avoid them and plan towards getting the future you desire.

Do you picture yourself in heaven for all eternity? Do you see yourself walking on the streets of gold with all the saints and your loved ones? There will be no more separation, sickness, deformity, death, failure, pain, disappointment, tears, or sorrow. Wouldn't it feel great to giggle and dance with your departed dad, mum, spouse, sister, brother, child, and friend once again? This time with no morbid, impending fear of separation—never ever again. Would you spare an eternal minute to meet Father Abraham, King David, Mary (mother of Jesus), and Apostle Paul? They've heard so much about you and can't wait to meet you!

Do you see yourself singing praises to God under the Tree of Life, just by the crystal-clear River of Life, all the while beholding the splendour of God's throne? (Rev. 22:1–2). Can you imagine yourself free of all the sins and weights you struggle with down here? Imagine being free to worship God in all purity as you have always desired (Rev. 21:27). Do you see yourself sitting safely among the wolves and lambs as they quietly graze together? There, the lion eats straw like the ox, and dust is the serpent's food (Isa. 65:25).

> One of the lessons we can learn from this shrewd manager is to always live with eternity in view.

Yet all this is nothing more than just a glimpse of the glory God has in store for His saints. Listen to how Paul puts it: "Eye has not seen, nor ear heard, nor have entered into the heart of man the things which God has prepared for those who love Him" (1 Cor. 2:9).

Our best imaginations about heaven or hell will always fail us. Nothing can compare to the extremities of the two eternal destinations. However, the *little* the Bible reveals to us about both is enough to help us make our choice of where we would like to spend eternity. Even the dishonest manager was shrewd enough to choose comfort over pain. Are you?

Just like the shrewd manager desired a future of comfort and abundance, we can desire an eternal future of comfort, peace, joy, and glory. Though he went about it the wrong way, we can go about it the right way—and Jesus is *that* Way.

ACTIONS HAVE CONSEQUENCES

The shrewd manager tailored his actions to achieve his desired goals. Once he had decided on the future that he desired for himself, he identified how to live in the present to get the future of his dreams. People would not welcome him into their homes just because he wished for it. As the nursery rhyme goes, "If wishes were horses, beggars would ride. If if's and and's were pots and pans, there'd surely be dishes to do." Unfortunately for beggars, wishes are just wishes—at least until preparation meets opportunity.

The manager understood the principle of giving: *Give and it shall be given unto you.* If he wanted people to help him in his time of need, he had to help those people in their own time of need. How many people in positions of privilege lack this basic foresight? They use all their privileges to cater for only their needs without thinking about the possibility of the winds of fortune changing directions to their disadvantage. When out of such positions, they cannot point to anyone they helped when they had the means. In eternal things, it is also important for us to understand basic kingdom principles.

> *Like the dying king, many of us are good at making detailed plans for ephemeral things yet fail to prepare for our eternal destination.*

Fortunately for us, we don't have to resort to dishonest means like the manager. God's principles are in His Word and His Word is perfect.

If you desire to spend eternity in heaven, the Bible is filled with guidelines and principles on how to get there. If you want to be celebrated by Jesus Christ in heaven as a faithful servant who fed His sheep while here on earth, there are many guidelines provided in the Bible for that. But you must be willing and diligent enough to study the Word to know how to plan and prepare for your eternal destiny. Nobody stumbles into heaven or hell. We all make our choices here on earth—God simply confirms them, for all eternity.

A good Biblical principle that can guide us on our way to heaven is helping the poor and the needy. Jesus said if we desire to be welcome by Him in heaven with all pomp and pageantry, we should focus on feeding the hungry, giving drinks to the thirsty, visiting the sick, being hospitable to strangers, providing clothing for those in need, and visiting those in prison (Matt. 25:37–39). "I tell you the truth, when you did it to one of the least of these my brothers and sisters, you were doing it to me" (Matt. 25:40 NLT).

While it's good to desire eternity with God in heaven, the big question is: When last did we do any of the above? It's true that salvation doesn't come from good works, but our good works are evidence that we are saved. We cannot be saved and not have good works emanating from the newness of our transformed hearts. Apostle James captured this perfectly thus:

> Also faith by itself, if it does not have works, is dead. But someone will say, "You have faith, and I have works." Show me your faith without your works, and I will show you my faith by my works. (James 2:17–18)

STRATEGIC IN APPROACH

The shrewd manager was strategic in his approach to secure his desired future. He didn't directly tell the people who owed his master he had waived parts of their debts. Rather, he invited them "to come and discuss the situation" (v. 5). He understood human nature; people often take for granted what they get free or easily. We tend to measure, often subconsciously, the worth of a thing by how much we struggle to get it or pay for it.

Giving the debtors the debt relief without them soliciting it might diminish its worth in their eyes—or even got them wary of the manager. Contrary to our intuition, gratitude is not highly correlated with how much we have or have been given. Rather, gratitude is highly correlated with how much *we value* what we have or have been given. This may explain in part why we need to pray even though God already knows our desires. Praying helps to build anticipation in us, and then gratitude when God finally grants our desires.

> *Our best imaginations about heaven or hell will always fail us! Nothing can be compared to the extremities of the two eternal destinations.*

This human flaw is reflected in almost every aspect of our lives. For example, children growing up in affluent homes, with all their needs freely met, may not be as grateful as children who struggle to get by. Some resentment may be brewing in an affluent home over the wrong choice of colour for a car received as a birthday gift. In contrast, one may find the ebullience of shared love and laughter over a bowl of legumes shared by siblings who are thankful for not going to bed hungry.

Many a believer is blessed with a wonderful *and* imperfect spouse. But they fail to appreciate God's gift to them and may even feel shortchanged; they think they deserve better. They can't see the value of what they have, probably because God gave it to them without letting them trudge through many heartbreaks in the treacherous marketplace of dating.

They are quick to catalogue and emphasize their *immense* sacrifices and contributions to their marriage but become purblind when it comes to seeing and appreciating their partner's sacrifices. They keep digging the grave of their union with the spade of ingratitude until it's wide and deep enough to swallow them up—and then suddenly, they receive their perfect sight! This postmortem *wisdom* is proof that indeed hindsight is 20/20.

The church is not spared either. Many *broken* people in the church today didn't just join the church. They were initially part of the church but undervalued her authority, worth, and guidance until they finally left for the *real* world where, unfortunately, they got more than they bargained for. Contrite and broken, they returned to church to learn humbly what they had previously refused to learn. Many think the yoke of Christ

> **Nobody stumbles into heaven or hell. We all make our choices here on earth—God simply confirms them, for all eternity.**

is too heavy, until they try the yoke of the world. It seems they would only learn the hard way, but thank God for His mercy. He receives them back with love and joy, like the prodigal son.

The shrewd manager understood this human flaw well enough to not lay all his cards on the table. He needed some sort of assurance that the debtors would value and appreciate the largesse he was about to offer them. Not only did he want to *help* them (more like help himself), but he also wanted them to *know* he was doing them a favour—for that was only when they would be in his debt.

He probably gauged each debtor's level of interest before deciding on the magnitude of relief to offer. He understood the principle that

THE SHREWD MANAGER

he who is forgiven more, loves much (Luke 7:47)—provided they acknowledge that they have been forgiven more.

Do we value God's gifts enough to realize that we will forever be in His debt? His Word protects us from the world, but if we don't value it and learn from it, we will learn from the world the hard way. As a reminder, the world runs a very expensive school that sucks its students dry and leaves them empty. We clearly see that in the parable of the prodigal son. He didn't value what he had at home until he got schooled by the pigs abroad. He came back begging in rags for what he once had on a platter of gold.

Parents would do well to apply this strategy in training their children to be more grateful for all the *blessings* they receive. Gratitude is one of the greatest assets parents can give to their children. They should be taught very early in life the value of money and what it takes to put food on the table. Entitled children may struggle with relationships later in life, even into adulthood. Gratitude may be the least of all virtues, but ingratitude is one of the worst vices. Parents should therefore pray for wisdom to raise their children in such a manner that they won't grow up into entitled adults who take people and things for granted.

ACTING IN FAITH

The shrewd manager acted in faith. There were no guarantees that the debtors he helped would return the favour. Though he took reasonable caution, it was still a risk. There's no mention in the parable that both parties signed an undertaking that they would repay him in kind. If they chose not to repay him, he could not drag them to court to enforce the breach.

He who comes into equity must come with clean hands. The dishonest manager obviously had very dirty fingers. His actions were both illegal and bad conduct. Thus, there would have been no legal recourse for him, yet he took the chance. He didn't wait for everything to be perfect before he acted. "Farmers who wait for perfect weather never plant. If they watch every cloud, they never harvest" (Eccles. 11:4 NLT).

If you wait till all your needs are met before you give to the needy, you may never give. If you wait until all the problems in your life disappear before you help others, you may never help. You must step out in faith, trusting God to take good care of you. Many wait to be watered before they water others. They got the order wrong. "The generous soul will be made rich, and he who waters will also be watered himself" (Prov. 11:25). You must water first, then you will be watered—and that's an act of faith.

> We cannot be saved and not have good works emanating from the newness of our transformed hearts.

Like the widow who gave all she had (Luke 21: 1–4), we need to learn to act in faith if we want to see more of God's miracles in our lives. Many families are praying for financial breakthrough but have never prioritized helping those in greater needs than they are. They use their needs as justification for not helping others. They fail to realize that they may be the ones holding back their own blessings.

The Bible says, "Give and it will be given unto you" (Luke 6:38 NIV). It doesn't say, "Give when you have a lot or an excess." Give right where you are. I remember the story of three friends who exemplified this act of love and faith. Brother A was in financial straits when he got a call from his friend, Brother B, who told him he hadn't eaten anything that day. Brother A had nothing to give to his friend, but his heart sincerely wanted to help. Later in the week, a mutual friend, Brother C, sent Brother A an amount of money that could barely meet his need. But rather than justifiably spend all the pittance on himself, Brother A split it into equal halves and sent one half to Brother B. The three friends didn't have millions to share, yet they shared the little they had.

> Contrary to our intuition, gratitude is not highly correlated with how much we have or have been given. Rather, gratitude is highly correlated with how much we value what we have or have been given.

When you have nothing to give, God checks your heart. Whatever is in your heart, God can place in your hands. But if you are not faithful with the little you have, you will probably not be faithful with much. It takes faith to give with no hope of getting anything in return. Yet God wants you to

> cast your bread upon the waters. For you will find it after many days. Give a serving to seven, and also to eight. For you do not know what evil will be on the earth. (Eccles. 11:1–2)

GODLY WISDOM OR EARTHLY SHREWDNESS?

Believers often express their shock at how quickly evil seems to have taken over the world. Of course, they know it's the devil's handiwork. But how did it happen so fast? What are the mechanisms of this plunge into the swirling rapids of perversion? Jesus provides the answer in this parable: "The children of this world [unbelievers] are more shrewd in dealing with the world around them than are the children of the light [Christians]" (v. 8). The moral depravity in the world today is not some tragic accident. It is carefully planned, orchestrated, and driven towards a definite end.

Unbelievers often pursue their purposes and ideologies not just with *religious* fervour, but also with well-thought-out strategies. Long before their ideas become popular, they've been *cooked and recooked* behind the scenes. When released into the world, we wonder how something *that new* could take over the world so quickly. Well, maybe it's not *that new*.

They may use benevolent causes and charitable organizations as fronts to cover up their actual agendas. Even in their wills, some make endowments to leading universities for the financial support of their ideologies—in a way, posthumously recruiting the best minds in the world in that pursuit.

While the church often focuses on adults and treats children simply as children, the world sees these children as the future. So, they focus on indoctrinating them with their ideologies as early as possible. Soon enough, the children, now young adults, rise as a socio-political tsunami to change the social and political landscapes of the society. At that point, the *righteous elders* in the church can only protest in righteous indignation within the confining walls of their churches. This shows a lack of insight and foresight.

In choosing Abraham, God prioritized his ability to transmit the divine knowledge to his children:

> I have singled him out so that he will direct his sons and their families to keep the way of the LORD by doing what is right and just. *Then* I will do for Abraham all that I have promised. (Gen. 18:19 NLT, emphasis mine)

The fulfillment of God's promise to Abraham that he would be great and become a great nation was contingent on him having children and descendants who obeyed God and were worthy carriers of the covenant. That would only happen if Abraham taught his children God's commandments. His life exemplified the Biblical injunction to learn God's commandments and to

> repeat them again and again to your children. Talk about them when you are at home and when you are on the road, when you are going to bed and when you are getting up. (Deut. 6:7 NLT)

The world has mastered the art and science of indoctrinating children, using means such as cartoons, apps, social media, games, *children's* movies, schoolbooks, and summer camps. No stone is left unturned.

A child at home may be indoctrinated with ungodly ideas via social media and digital entertainments right under the parent's nose. You would be worried if you got home one day and saw your children playing with strangers in their bedrooms. Yet this is often the case—digitally. Our children may be digitally engaging with strangers from all around the world right in their bedrooms. These have now become the strangers in our homes.

In choosing Abraham, God prioritized his ability to transmit the divine knowledge to his children.

Many churches struggle to find committed and innovative teachers for their children's Sunday schools. Rather than ask God for wisdom to engage and serve faithfully in His vineyard, believers often just complain about the pervasiveness of evil in the world. We curse the darkness rather than turn on the light.

Think about just one thing you can do to contribute to the propagation of God's kingdom here on earth and follow through with it. A God-inspired action, no matter how small, is better than a torrent of complaints.

There's wisdom for every situation, no matter how daunting it seems. Apostle Paul displayed wisdom several times during his ministry. One time, while in Athens, he brilliantly presented the gospel to a hostile community by telling them he was introducing to them "the Unknown God" to whom they had already raised an altar.

The idolatrous Athenians had raised an altar to *the unknown God*, probably to cover all bases, in case they had missed out on one of their numerous gods. Paul's logic was: "You call Him 'an unknown God,' and I'm here to tell you more about Him." That's wisdom in action.

> For as I was walking along, I saw many shrines. And one of your altars had this inscription on it: "To the Unknown God." This God, whom you worship without knowing, is the one I'm telling you about. (Acts 17:23 NLT)

In another instance, when he was standing trial before a hostile Sanhedrin (high council), on realizing that some of them were Sadducees while the others were Pharisees, he brought up the issue of the resurrection of the dead, which he knew the two groups sharply disagreed on.

> *A God-inspired action, no matter how small, is better than a torrent of complaints. There's wisdom for every situation.*

It worked. There was a great uproar, and the council broke into division as the Pharisees felt Paul didn't deserve to die just because he preached about his hope in the resurrection of the dead (Acts 23:6–10). As a result, he was whisked off to the safety of the barracks.

God did not castigate Paul for using this wisdom to save himself. Rather, the following night, Jesus appeared to him, stood near him, and said, "Take courage! As you have testified about me in Jerusalem, so you must also testify in Rome" (Acts 23:11 NIV). Note that in his applications of wisdom, Paul neither lied nor denied Jesus Christ. There's godly wisdom for every situation.

USING THE UNRIGHTEOUS MAMMON TO MAKE ETERNAL FRIENDS

On October 28, 1949, Jim Elliot, the martyred Christian missionary, scribbled in his journal the following words: "He is no fool who gives [to God] what he cannot keep to gain [from God] that which he cannot lose."[1] Interestingly, next to the statement, he quoted Luke

16:9, a verse from the current parable: "That when it shall fail, they may receive you into everlasting habitations."

Hundreds of years earlier, the English nonconformist preacher Phillip Henry (1631–1696), the father of Matthew Henry (1662–1714), the famous Bible commentator, had written a similar statement: "He is no fool who parts with that which he cannot keep, when he is sure to be recompensed with that which he cannot lose."[2]

Money has wings and can fly away, but our eternal treasure is forever secure. Like the shrewd manager, we should use our worldly resources to benefit others and make friends. Then, *when* our possessions are gone, they will welcome us to an eternal home.

The safest bank in the world is probably the growling stomachs of the hungry and the empty hands of the needy. These are direct conduits to our heavenly bank deposit. The shrewd manager used his master's money to buy friends for himself. We can also use our Master's money and resources to build up treasure for ourselves in heaven and make heavenly friends to welcome us when we get to that point where earthly money holds no value.

> *The safest bank in the world is probably the growling stomachs of the hungry and the empty hands of the needy.*

We will all surely get to that point when all our earthly possessions will be gone—either they leave us, or we leave them. One way or another, our possessions will be gone one day. Heaven eagerly awaits the arrival of the saints who take care of the needy on earth. The saints who have been touched by our generosity on earth will also reunite with us in heaven, with gratitude. This is the smartest way to convert the unrighteous mammon (money) into real riches and heavenly friends.

Givers are God's creditors, and He pays back with unimaginably high interests. "He who has pity on the poor lends to the LORD, and He will pay back what he has given" (Prov. 19:17). Now we know why the hypocritical Pharisees, who loved money, sneered at Jesus after hearing this parable.

Chapter 11

THE PEARL
&
THE HIDDEN
TREASURE

The Kingdom of Heaven is like a treasure that a man discovered hidden in a field. In his excitement, he hid it again and sold everything he owned to get enough money to buy the field. Again, the Kingdom of Heaven is like a merchant on the lookout for choice pearls. When he discovered a pearl of great value, he sold everything he owned and bought it!

MATTHEW 13:44–46 (NLT)

There was once a wealthy widower who had everything—well, almost everything—he ever wanted: gold coins; houses spread across choice parts of town; and thousands of cattle, donkeys, horses, and camels. He had hundreds of slaves who served him as domestics or worked on his many plantations. Kings and other powerful rulers were at his beck and call. He was indeed a powerful and influential man. He had lost his beloved wife years earlier and had chosen to remain single, focusing all his attention on their only child, a son, and his many businesses.

On the tenth anniversary of his wife's death, he became seriously ill and died shortly afterward. Traditionally, all his wealth would go to his son, but he left a will—a troubling will. He specified in his will that his most trusted slave, not his son, should receive all his wealth. But a clause in the will allowed his son to take only one item from his estate before the rest was transferred to the trusted slave.

Understandably, the devastating news left the son in despair. It wasn't just about the loss of property, but it felt like his father neither had love for him nor confidence in his ability to manage his estate. He must have thought so little of him to have preferred to hand over all his inheritance to a slave. He was angry that his father had brought him public ridicule and shame.

He was, however, also pragmatic. He knew a bleak future was staring him right in the face, and he needed to act fast. Despite his protest, the will of his father was inviolable and must be honoured. He could choose one item in accordance with his father's will, or choose nothing in protest.

On his part, the trusted slave could not believe his good fortune. From a lowly slave to the richest man in town! He felt a bit sorry for the son, but he wasn't about to miss a golden opportunity to escape a life of poverty and servitude. His dressing changed, and his strides became more elegant. His network of friends expanded exponentially, and influential individuals who previously wouldn't have acknowledged his existence now shamelessly courted him, treating him as their most cherished companion.

All the while, the son was abandoned, even by his theretofore best friends. In a last bid to save himself from a lifetime of misery and shame, he started visiting his late father's close friends to seek advice. He wanted to know if his father had confided in any of them about why he hated him so much that he gave his inheritance to a slave.

None of his father's friends could help him. They were all equally shocked at the behaviour of their late friend. Finally, the son went to see an elderly recluse in a neglected part of town. He went to him weeping but left with a poker face. Nobody knew what he discussed with the old recluse that made his countenance change.

On the day scheduled for the official reading of the will, the arena was filled with a crowd eager to witness this spectacle of a slave turned heir apparent. All the documents of the late man's estate were placed on a table. If the son chose one of them, it would be only one item. If he chose a house, it would be just the house and nothing else. Whereas the slave was the best dressed attendee at the occasion, the son—probably in anticipation of his bleak future—was dressed like a pauper.

The son was called to announce publicly which of his late father's property he would like to choose so that the rest could be handed over to the slave, who was standing right beside him. All eyes were fixed on the unfortunate son. Some in pity; some in disgust. After all, his father wouldn't have treated him this way had he been a good lad—or so they thought.

Without looking at the crowd, he could feel their intense gazes piercing right through him. As he hobbled towards the table holding the documents, the anticipation reached a fever pitch. There was silence everywhere. It was as if no one was breathing. You could hear a pin drop in the arena.

He paused right in front of the table, muttering something to himself as he looked intently at the documents. If only his intense gaze could merge all the documents into one for him to pick! No such miracle occurred. He stole a glance at the silent crowd for a moment, and then began to walk back to his previous position—without picking any item from the table.

"The poor lad must have chosen to protest his father's wickedness by refusing to pick any item," many in the crowd thought. When he got back to his former position, he stood right in front of the slave, *the pretender to his throne*, as if to plead with him one last time. He gently, but firmly, placed his right hand on the slave's left shoulder, looked him right in the eye, and said calmly, "I choose you!"

The slave was shell-shocked. It took a while for it all to sink in. According to the tradition of the time, slaves were chattels, and they belonged to their masters. So, the son had just chosen one item from his father's property—his most trusted slave. He who owns the slave owns all the slave owns. It didn't matter what else was bequeathed to the slave. All ultimately belonged to the son.

The son had just delivered to the crowd a masterclass in shrewdness. But it wasn't his wisdom; it was the wisdom of the old recluse whom he had visited. Maybe his father was not a monster after all. He just wanted him to learn how to seek wise counsel. If he was wise enough to seek counsel and make the right decisions, he would be wise enough to manage his newly found wealth. "Where there is no counsel, the people fall; but in the multitude of counselors there is safety" (Prov. 11:14).

THE CHIEF TREASURE

The story above can be summed up by one Bible verse: "But seek ye first the kingdom of God and His righteousness, and all these things shall be added to you" (Matt. 6:33). Like the son of the wealthy man in the story, we often struggle with the dilemma of choosing the most important thing from what seems to be an array of equally important things. We juggle the responsibilities of relationships, career, health, finance, ministry, and so on. It feels like we are being pulled in a million different directions by forces beyond our control. We have so many things to do but very little time to do them all.

"You must prioritize!" they say, but we are not sure which pursuit we can, or should, allow to suffer. We must work to provide for our families, but they still need our time and attention—yet work takes most of our time. It feels like a rat race run in a vicious cycle, which everyone says is bad, but from which no one seems to know how to get away, while still catering to our legitimate needs.

Bills, bills, and then … more bills; everywhere we look, we see bills. Utilities, tuition fees, childcare, mortgages, rents, credit cards, grocery, taxes, loans, insurance payments, car finance, gas, and so on. Bills, like a relentless wolf pack, keep chasing us for the greater part of our lives. It's easy to be overwhelmed by all this and other challenges of life.

We can get so distracted, just like Martha (Luke 10:41), that we hardly can spare a moment of quiet to sit at the feet of Jesus. Even when we manage to spare some minutes for *quiet time*, our minds are everywhere, except on prayer and meditation. Quiet time is no longer quiet. Sadly, this is how billions of people live daily, too busy to make time for their relationship with God. Tragically, many die amid these pursuits.

In Matthew 6:33, Jesus revealed a great insight into how we can make the most of our time here on earth by telling us what to prioritize above all else. Unlike in the situation of the son in the story above, even if we are allowed to choose more than one item from our earthly pursuits, we will still miss out on a lot. Choosing the kingdom of God is like choosing the most trusted slave: with it comes *all* other things. Only this treasure can single-handedly meet all the diverse needs of the human soul.

Ambitions and achievements may at first bring a sense of fulfillment and pride, but these fade with time, and we sense some emptiness within. Sometimes, our achievements are anticlimactic. This feels like reaching a summit only to discover it doesn't feel as great as we had fantasized all along—but we feign proportionate, or even exaggerated, happiness because that's what is expected of us. Worse still, these achievements can easily slip through our fingers or be rendered obsolete by the fast pace of the modern world and the chameleonic nature of human relationships.

Nothing that can be taken away from you is truly yours: money, life, health, spouse, and so on. Mary wisely chose that which would not be taken away from her—God's kingdom and His righteousness (Luke 10:42). As we go about our daily pursuits, we should not forget the words of Jesus to Martha, *the patron saint of busy humans*:

> And Jesus answered and said to her, "Martha, Martha, you are worried and troubled about many things. But one thing is needed, and Mary has chosen that good part, which will not be taken away from her." (Luke 10:41–42)

Jesus didn't say Martha was not busy. She was busy but had neglected the most important thing in her life: the state of her soul. As much as Jesus appreciated all the preparations Martha was making in His honour, He cared more for her soul than His own comfort. He wanted the best for her, not for Himself. He called her affectionately, even twice, "Martha, Martha," to get her attention and take her gaze off her busy schedule. Hush … hush … can you hear it? Can you hear the same voice calling out to you with the same affection as you go about your busy schedule? His feet are still warm, and you can find solace there.

Even when we manage to spare some minutes for quiet time, our minds are everywhere, except on prayer and meditation. Quiet time is no longer quiet.

Our appetites for the things of this world may cloud our judgment and blind us to their ephemeral nature. We work to feed ourselves. Yet one day, both the stomach and the food will be no more. "Foods for the stomach and the stomach for foods, but God will destroy both it and them" (1 Cor. 6:13). All the well-fed people of yesteryear are dust in the ground now, just like their poorly-fed contemporaries. They took nothing with them. We should cater for our mundane needs, but not at the expense of our souls.

> For what will it profit a man if he gains the whole world, and loses his own soul? Or what will a man give in exchange for his soul? (Mark 8:36–37)

THE KINGDOM OF HEAVEN AS A TREASURE

We have the tendency to estimate the value of a thing by how much it costs us in terms of effort or money. When we get things easily or for free, we tend not to appreciate them. There is nothing we can offer God in exchange for the gift of His kingdom. So, He gave it to us freely. And that's why many believers do not appreciate the gift of the kingdom of heaven. It is a treasure of inestimable worth. It's free, but it's not cheap. It's free because someone has borne all the cost.

It is commonplace to see believers, especially those born into Christian homes, behave as if they are the ones doing God a favour by being believers. They often preface their statements with: "If not for Jesus, I would have …." Not uttered with a sense of gratitude, but as if Jesus has placed an irritating restriction on them. As if He is restraining them from doing what is best for them. They act as if they are the sacrificial lamb, not Jesus Christ. They feel they could handle their lives better, if only Jesus would let them be.

This attitude differs totally from that of the apostles when Jesus asked them if they also wanted to abandon Him like His other followers just did. John described the situation like this:

> From that time many of His disciples went back and walked with Him no more. Then Jesus said to the twelve, "Do you also want to go away?" But Simon Peter answered Him, "Lord, to whom shall we go? You have the words of eternal life. And we have come to believe and know that You are the Christ, the Son of the living God." (John 6:66–69)

If many modern ministers face what Jesus experienced when many of His disciples abandoned Him, they would have tried their best to retain their few remaining members, even at the expense of telling them the truth. The remnant members, sensing the desperation of their ministers, may also take advantage of the situation to make unreasonable demands and do as they please.

In contrast, Jesus, rather than grovel before the remaining disciples, asked them point-blank, "Do you also want to go away?" Jesus did this to underscore the great value of the kingdom of heaven. It is not something to dole out to unwilling and unappreciative recipients. Those who will possess it must know its worth. Jesus put it this way:

> Do not give what is holy to the dogs; nor cast your pearls before swine, lest they trample them under their feet, and turn and tear you in pieces. (Matt. 7:6)

The kingdom of heaven is a precious treasure that must not be wasted on people who do not value or appreciate it. Jesus further emphasized the worth of His kingdom by advising His audience to give all in their capacity to enter it, to the point of losing their *eye* or *leg*, if need be. The eye and leg are symbolic of the things so precious to us that we can't imagine living without them. He said,

> And if your eye causes you to sin, pluck it out and cast it from you. It is better for you to enter into life with one eye, rather than having two eyes, to be cast into hell fire. (Matt. 18:9)

Believers with terrible pasts or converts from other faiths often display a level of zeal and gratitude for their salvation than is generally observed in believers born into Christian homes and raised in a *decent* manner. It seems the former appreciate the gift of God's salvation more, as they can easily contrast their newfound life in Christ with their very dark pasts. In contrast, the latter might have been spared the negative consequences of riotous living and may not have a frame of reference to which they could contrast the glorious liberty they currently enjoy in the kingdom. They may think they've never been *that bad* throughout their lives. Or they may even long for some *action* which they feel their pious upbringing has deprived them. Thus, they may struggle with gratitude in their walk with God.

Of course, this observation is not universally applicable, and there is nothing wrong with being born into a Christian home and being raised in the way of the Lord. In fact, it's the desire of many godly parents. However, we should be wary of getting so used to the blessing of our salvation that we lose our wonders of God.

That God doesn't always reveal to us what He saves us from shouldn't make us take His protection for granted. We mustn't suffer broken jaws before we value the protective shields God has placed around us. It's a privilege and an honour to have the Almighty God as our bodyguard. Let us accept this honour with profound respect and utmost gratitude.

One day, Jesus was reminiscing on how blessed His disciples were for being freely given the mystery of the kingdom. The disciples themselves probably didn't know at that point how blessed they were. Notice the wonder and gratitude in Jesus' speech recorded in the book of Matthew as follows:

> I thank You, Father, Lord of heaven and earth, that You have hidden these things from the wise and prudent and have released them to babes. Even so, Father, for so it seemed good in Your sight. (Matt. 11:25–26)

God wants us to always celebrate the inheritance we have in Him. Yet many of us keep groaning and complaining about how much sacrifice we are making for the sake of the kingdom. We make it sound like we are the ones doing God a favour.

About 167,000 people die each day around the world.[1] That is about 115 deaths every minute (two deaths every second). Of this number, many go into eternity away from God, but believers face death with the assurance of eternal bliss with God. No matter how hard their earthly lives have been, they have a prospect of eternal joy ahead of them. If that is not enough reason to be thankful for the gift of salvation, what else is? Even in their lifetimes, they have God as their Father, Friend, and Lover.

> *Nothing that can be taken away from you is truly yours: money, life, health, spouse, and so on.*

While the wise and powerful people of this world grope in the dark trying to find the meaning of life and the secret of happiness, God's children have it all revealed to them in His Word. Glory! Hallelujah! The Holy Spirit of God freely reveals these secrets to *babes*, His children. We must learn to count our blessings daily and find reasons to be grateful to God for the wonderful treasure of His kingdom.

THE KINGDOM OF GOD IS HIDDEN BUT CAN BE DISCOVERED

As shown in these twin parables, in a sense, the kingdom of God, like all treasures, is not lying carelessly by the roadside. It is hidden away from the prying eyes of passers-by. It is hidden in the ground. Who knows how many times the man had ploughed that field in every direction without knowing he was walking on a treasure that could change his life forever?

Have you heard some sermons so many times that you can now complete the preacher's sentences? I have. Yet that doesn't mean we have found the treasures in those sermons. It simply means we have ploughed the field several times. We do not know the truth until it has set us free. We merely know about it, ploughing the surface, but we have yet to strike gold.

Do we even realize how deep and plenteous the treasures in Christ are? "In Him lie hidden all the treasures of wisdom and knowledge" (Col. 2:3 NLT). All we need for life and godliness is already provided and hidden in Christ. The diligent soul will not rest until it uncovers and claims these treasures, just like the man and the merchant in these parables.

We often miss great treasures because they are covered or buried in dirt. The Jews and the Greeks missed Jesus because He didn't meet their expectations. Both the Jews and the Greeks considered the notion of Jesus as the Messiah equally preposterous. The Jews wanted signs as proof of His Messiahship, while the Greeks wanted a flamboyant display of human wisdom. "It is foolish to the Jews, who ask for signs from heaven. And it is foolish to the Greeks, who seek human wisdom" (1 Cor. 1:22 NLT).

Jesus disappointed both groups as He showed them neither the signs nor the human wisdom they expected. They missed the treasure because it did not come in the form they expected. Rather than show up on the world's greatest throne as a wise and mighty conqueror,

> He grew up before Him like a tender shoot, and like a root out of a dry ground. He had no beauty or majesty to attract us to Him, nothing in His appearance that we should desire Him. (Isa. 53:2)

We must be ready to dig through the dirt if we are to unravel the beauty of the treasures lying underneath. We must not let the god of this age blind us to our wealth in Christ or let ourselves be hoodwinked into valuing the dirt more than the treasures. If human adulation is the dirt, get rid of it. If greed is the dirt, dig it out of your life until the glorious treasures shine through. No dirt should be too precious for us to dig out to reach the underlying treasures.

Many miss out on godly spouses loaded with God's treasures just because they do not come in the form or manner they expect. The women who married Noah's sons never knew they just made a decision that would one day save their lives. Blessings often come in disguise, with layers of dirt that may need to be scraped off. Ask God to help you get rid of the dirt so that you can see and appreciate the underlying treasure.

Dirt also often comes in disguise, with a veneer of gold concealing its bulk of dross. You cannot marry dirt and expect a treasure. Scrape it all you want; you'll only reveal more dirt. It takes God, and not mere willpower, to transform dirt to treasure. Let's learn to value God's treasures in ourselves and others. That way, we won't be easily deceived by dirt masquerading as treasure.

> *However, we should be wary of getting so used to the blessing of our salvation that we lose our wonders of God.*

While the Jews and Greeks missed out on Jesus, the disciples stayed with Him until they saw through the *dirt* of His humble background and mien. They soon discovered the inestimable worth of God's kingdom in Him. From lowly fishermen, they became the pillars of the church, have their names inscribed on the twelve foundations of the wall of the heavenly Jerusalem (Rev. 21:14), and will sit on twelve thrones to judge the twelve tribes of Israel in eternity (Matt. 19:28). That's not a bad deal at all.

When Jesus called His disciples, He didn't furnish them with the details of all the treasures they would eventually possess. For most of them, He focused on telling them their future assignment, rather than their reward: "Follow Me, and I will make you fishers of men. They immediately left their nets and followed Him" (Matt. 4:19–20). They left their earthly fortune and relationships behind to follow Him, with no firm assurances of what they would get in return—no job offer letters outlining their compensations and benefits.

This was such a great sacrifice that many people who thronged around Jesus declined to follow Him. Who would want to leave all comfort behind to follow the Son of Man who had nowhere to lay His head?

> Now it happened as they journeyed on the road, that someone said to Him, "Lord, I will follow You wherever You go." And Jesus said to him, "Foxes have holes and birds of the air have nests, but the Son of Man has nowhere to lay His head." Then He said to another, "Follow Me." But he said, "Lord, permit me first to go and bury my father." Jesus said to him, "Let the dead bury their own dead, but you go and preach the kingdom of God." (Luke 9:57–60)

There is always a price to pay to follow Jesus. By nature, the kingdom of God suffers violence and the violent take it by force (Matt. 11:12). Some like Zacchaeus had to climb a tree just to catch a glimpse of Jesus (Luke 19:1–10). When Jesus withdrew into a boat, an eager crowd followed on foot to hear Him teach (Matt. 14:13). Many followed and stayed with Him for three days with nothing to eat (Matt. 15:32). The disciples gave their all just to be with Him (Matt. 19:27). These people did not leave their salvation to chance; they took the kingdom by force. What sacrifices have you made to lay hold on the kingdom of God? Are you ready to "fight the good fight of faith, [and] lay hold on eternal life"? (1 Tim. 6:12).

That God doesn't always reveal to us what He saves us from shouldn't make us take His protection for granted.

Many people today claim they are non-religious because they find it stressful to determine which religion is true among the many in the world. Yet these people spend years of their lives in school studying to acquire academic degrees or learn a trade. The materials they study in their first year of college, combined, are often more voluminous than the entire Bible, which contains about 783,137 words (the Authorized King James Version).[2]

If we can apply ourselves to acquiring academic degrees or learning a trade, then it shouldn't be too difficult for us to search for the truth on matters of life, purpose, death, and eternity. We can make time to read at least some portions of the Bible. Just reading through any of the Gospels could reveal some truths to the sincere seeker. It is our responsibility to search for the truth. Eternity is too long to be treated nonchalantly.

The Bible says, "Buy the truth, and do not sell it, also wisdom and instructions and understanding" (Prov. 23:23). This implies we should value truth and wisdom as priceless treasures, more valuable than rubies. We must diligently search for the truth and hold on to it (Jer. 29:13; John 8:31). Hear Job's euphonic praise of wisdom:

> But where can wisdom be found? And where is the place of understanding? Man does not know its value, nor is it found in the land of the living. The deep says, "It's not in me"; and the sea says, "It's not with me." It cannot be purchased for gold, nor can silver be weighed for its price. It cannot be valued in the gold of Ophir, in precious onyx or sapphire. Neither gold or crystal can equal it, nor can it be exchanged for jewelry of fine gold. No mention shall be made of coral or quartz, for the price of wisdom is above rubies. (Job. 28:12–18)

THE KINGDOM OF GOD COSTS EVERYTHING

The kingdom of God is so precious that it costs us everything. The man and the merchant in the parables both sold *everything* they owned to raise enough money to purchase the treasures they just found. But I mentioned earlier that the kingdom was offered to us free of charge. So why are we discussing cost now? The worth of the kingdom is so much more than whatever sacrifice we could ever make for it.

Think of it this way: Our everything is nothing compared to His everything. It's like a pauper exchanging his *all* for his king's *all*—those are on two totally different scales. Compare what the disciples gave up with what they got in return. They gave up their weather-beaten wooden fishing boats and got incorruptible gold thrones instead. They gave up their earthly families and friends to gain billions of families and friends in the Lord. They gave

> We often miss great treasures because they are covered or buried in dirt. The Jews and the Greeks missed Jesus because He didn't meet their expectations.

up their lives—with all its limitations—to gain everlasting life which no one can take from them.

Many believers wonder why they haven't experienced the fullness of God's promises in their lives. Maybe it's because they manage their faith in a manner that does not cost them anything, let alone everything. They practise their faith with extreme caution or apathy. Theirs is not a faith that drives them into action. It is not a fire in their bones. They are not like the saints of old, not like Apostle Paul or Prophet Jeremiah. The latter expressed his passion for God's kingdom when he said,

> Then I said, "I will not make mention of Him, nor speak anymore in His name." But His word was in my heart like a burning fire shut up in my bones; I was weary of holding it back, and I could not. (Jer. 20:9)

Jeremiah could not manage his faith in a cute, tidy manner. It was the driving force of his life. Similarly, Apostle Paul did not see any reason for him to be celebrated for preaching the gospel. It was his responsibility and a necessity for his survival. Hear him speak about it:

> For though I preach the gospel, I have nothing to glory of: for necessity is laid upon me; yea, woe is unto me, if I preach not the gospel! For if I do this thing willingly, I have a reward: but if against my will, a dispensation of the gospel is committed unto me. (1 Cor. 9:16–17 KJV)

> Yes, everything else is worthless when compared with the infinite value of knowing Christ Jesus my Lord. For His sake I have discarded everything else, counting it all as garbage, so that I could gain Christ. (Phil. 3:8 NLT)

Jeremiah and Paul did not serve God half-heartedly. For the sake of the kingdom, they gave their all—and ultimately their lives. Half commitment to the kingdom of heaven is like a person standing at a bus stop. If he stays away from the bus, he may be safe. If he gets on the bus, he may be safe. But if he puts one foot on the bus and the other on the ground, he is definitely *not* going to be safe. He risks serious injury or even death. We should be either hot or cold, not confusingly lukewarm.

Of the three conditions: the hot, the cold, and the lukewarm, the lukewarm is the most precarious spiritual state. Everyone knows the cold needs help to warm up. The hot will easily get help to maintain its warmth. But it's difficult to identify the need of the lukewarm as it varies unpredictably. Ultimately, the lukewarm will be discarded, not for being cold or hot, but for being unpredictable and dishonest. "So then, because you are lukewarm, and neither cold nor hot, I will vomit you out of My mouth" (Rev. 3:16). Jesus is either the Lord of all or the Lord of none. He is not the Lord of some parts of our lives. He wants to be the Lord of every part. He shouldn't be just a resident of our hearts, but the president thereof.

> *No dirt should be too precious for us to dig out to reach the underlying treasures.*

If you stay too long in the shower, it's probably because the water is lukewarm. If the water is either too cold or hot, you will probably jump out of the shower the moment it hits your body. Similarly, lukewarm believers make the church and the world conducive to ungodly activities and entities. When believers are on fire for God, ungodly activities melt away in their presence. There's a good reason you don't find flies forming a quorum on hot surfaces.

The same analogy applies to churches. Sinners and seekers may find a cold or hot church unsettling, but they may feel very much at home in a lukewarm church. Some churches are so much like the world in their dealings that even unbelievers get shocked when they visit such churches. An acquaintance once told me he left a church because it felt like a nightclub—he was an agnostic. He visited the church to *check out* the Christian faith but was so disappointed at how much the church was trying to imitate the worldliness outside. Well, I suspect he would have found a reason to leave a *hot* church too, maybe for being too fanatical or holier-than-thou. But a lukewarm church is *welcoming* to all: "Come as you are

> *It is our responsibility to search for the truth. Eternity is too long to be treated nonchalantly.*

and feel free to remain that way. We shall not rock thy boat in any way." A lukewarm church ensures the sinner's ride to hell is as smooth as possible.

There should be no middle ground in our commitment to the kingdom. Like King David, let us make up our minds not to give to God that which costs us nothing.

> Then the King said to Araunah, "No, I will surely buy it from you for a price; nor will I offer burnt offerings to the LORD my God with that which costs me nothing." (2 Sam. 24:24)

THERE IS COMPETITION FOR THE KINGDOM OF GOD

Just like other great treasures, there is competition for the kingdom of God. Several parties may be interested in a treasure for different reasons. These treasure hunters often compete to find treasures and retrieve artifacts for their market values. That is why the man who found the treasure in this parable buried it again while he went to raise the money to purchase it. He knew other people would be interested in it.

Many things compete for the kingdom of God in our lives: relationships, career, entertainment, health, wealth, and so on. Therefore, we must do our due diligence to jealously guard the kingdom. We must not allow anything to take the place of God in our hearts. Jesus warned us thus:

> If you want to be my disciple, you must, by comparison, hate everyone else—your father and mother, wife and children, brothers and sisters, even your own life. Otherwise, you cannot be my disciple. (Luke 14:26 NLT)

Jesus was not advocating hate or despicable treatment of ourselves or our families. After all, the Bible commands us to love one another (John 13:34) and honour our parents (Exo. 20:12). He was simply telling us the truth about how precious God should be to us. Our love for Him should be so intense that every other love pales in comparison and seems like *hate*. For example, many passionate believers have been accused by their loved ones of not loving them enough, simply because they appear to love God *too much*.

It is true that some believers neglect the needs of their family. These believers should remember that he who does not provide for his home is worse than an infidel (1 Tim. 5:8). However, in some instances, many loved ones emotionally manipulate devout believers into prioritizing them over God. Jesus experienced a similar situation. "When His family heard what was happening, they tried to take Him away. 'He's out of His mind,' they said" (Mark 3:21 NLT).

Jesus' family called Him *mad* and wanted to take Him into custody, just because He was so busy doing the will of God that He didn't even have time to eat. Later, His mother and brothers wanted to take Him away amid a ministration, but He told the crowd that His mothers and brothers are the ones who do the will of His Father in heaven (Mark 3:31–35). His mother and brothers could have felt offended by His statement and assumed He hated them. Yet He is love Himself. He loved His mother so much that even while dying on the Cross, He looked upon Her with love and made provision for her care, committing all her needs to His beloved disciple, John (John 19:26–27).

> *They practise their faith with extreme caution or apathy. Theirs is not a faith that drives them into action. It is not a fire in their bones.*

We should not seek to compete for the place of God in the lives of our loved ones. That's not love; it's emotional manipulation. Many parents disowned their children simply because the children accepted Jesus as their Lord and Saviour. To those parents, their children *hate* them just because they love the Lord. Similarly, many maltreat, abandon, or divorce their spouses simply because those spouses have become believers. Others lost their jobs or got *cancelled* for simply speaking out the truth in love. Some even lost their lives for the sake of the gospel. They loved not their lives even unto death (Rev. 12:11).

While some believers may be vacillating in their walk with God, others are giving their all to lay hold on the kingdom, for it is a great treasure. These devout believers will troop into heaven, from everywhere, even the ends of the earth. Jesus described it like this:

> There will be weeping and gnashing of teeth, when you see Abraham and Isaac and Jacob and all the prophets in the kingdom of God, and yourselves thrust out. They will come from the east and the west, from the north and the south, and sit down in the kingdom of God. (Luke 13:28–29)

Shall we spare a minute of sorrowful silence for the man who found the treasure, buried it, went away to sell his all, but got distracted along the way, and forgot all about it? Hope that is not you.

I leave you with these divinely inspired words of encouragement and hope from the mouth of Apostle Paul:

> Eye has not seen, nor ear heard, nor have entered into the heart of man the things which God has prepared for those who love Him. (1 Cor. 2:9)

> For our light affliction, which is but for a moment, is working for us a far more exceeding and eternal weight of glory. (2 Cor. 4:17)

ABOUT THE BOOK
VOLUME I
ও৶ও৶ও৶ও৶ও৶ও

The use of parables is rooted in the human affinity for story and storytelling. A well-delivered story builds anticipation in us and engages our imagination as the narrative progresses and the plot evolves until it reaches a crescendo. A story may serve as a seed for further conversation, thereby becoming a gift that keeps on giving. In the Bible, Jesus Christ skillfully used storytelling as a powerful vehicle for delivering eternal and timeless truths about God, grace, obedience, faith, stewardship, obedience, humility, prayer, heaven, hell, faithfulness, forgiveness, greed, wisdom, and many pertinent topics.

This volume digs deep to reveal the hidden gems in the following powerful parables told by Jesus Christ:

- The Wise and Foolish Builders
- The Mustard Seed
- The Wedding Banquet
- The Great Banquet
- The Sower
- The Growing Seed
- The Weeds
- The Yeast
- The Shrewd Manager
- The Pearl and the Hidden Treasure

ABOUT THE AUTHOR

Dami I. Olu has been a teacher of God's Word for more than 30 years. He has taught several congregations across Africa, Europe, and North America. His passion is to make the hidden treasures in the Bible accessible to all, regardless of academic or social status. He always seeks to highlight practical applications and timeless relevance of the Word to us today.

Notes

Introduction

1. Britannica, T. Editors of Encyclopaedia. "Epic of Gilgamesh." *Encyclopedia Britannica*, February 15, 2024. https://www.britannica.com/topic/Epic-of-Gilgamesh.

2. Jung, Carl G. *Man and his symbols*. Bantam, 2012.

Chapter 3: The Mustard Seed

1. Alfred Plummer. *An Exegetical Commentary on the Gospel According to St. Matthew*. New York: Scribner and Sons, 1909.

2. Kulp, Joshua. "English Explanation of Mishnah Tahorot 8:8." Accessed February 27, 2024. https://www.sefaria.org/Mishnah_Tahorot.8?lang=bi.

3. Kulp, Joshua. "English Explanation of Mishnah Kilayim 2:9." Accessed February 27, 2024. https://www.sefaria.org/Mishnah_Kilayim.2.9?lang=bi.

4. Woolston, Herbert. "Jesus Loves the Little Children." Accessed February 27, 2024. http://www.hymntime.com/tch/htm/j/e/s/l/jesloves.htm.

5. Stark, Rodney. *The Rise of Christianity: A sociologist reconsiders history*. Princeton University Press, 1996.

Chapter 4: The Wedding Banquet

1. Davidson, William. "Text from The William Davidson Digital Edition of the Koren Noé Talmud, with commentary by Rabbi Adin Even-Israel Steinsaltz." Accessed February 27, 2024. https://www.sefaria.org/Gittin.57b?lang=bi.

2. Davidson, William. "Text from The William Davidson Digital Edition of the Koren Noé Talmud, with commentary by Rabbi Adin Even-Israel Steinsaltz." Accessed February 27, 2024. https://www.sefaria.org/Sanhedrin.96b.6?lang=bi.

Chapter 8: The Weeds

1. Britannica, T. Editors of Encyclopaedia. "Spanish Inquisition | Key Facts | Britannica." n.d. Www.britannica.com. https://www.britannica.com/summary/Spanish-Inquisition-Key-Facts#:~:text=The%20Spanish%20Inquisition%20was%20a.

2. "Spanish Inquisition - New World Encyclopedia." 2019. Newworldencyclopedia.org. 2019. https://www.newworldencyclopedia.org/entry/Spanish_Inquisition.

3. Fagbemi, Tony (Nigeria, Guardian). 2022. "Bring Back Public Execution by Firing Squads." The Guardian Nigeria News - Nigeria and World News. September 23, 2022. https://guardian.ng/opinion/bring-back-public-execution-by-firing-squads/.

4. "Nigeria: Ten Thousand Watch as Three Robbers Are Executed in Public in Lagos (1971)." n.d. British Pathé. Accessed February 27, 2024. https://www.britishpathe.com/asset/128952/.

5. Okereke, Caleb & Kisesi, Patricia. "The Death Penalty Isn't African. It's a Legacy of Colonialism." Foreign Policy. https://foreignpolicy.com/2021/11/11/the-death-penalty-isnt-african-its-a-legacy-of-colonialism/.

6. Anthony Akinwale. "It's Not about SARS - by Rev. Prof. Anthony Akinwale." 2020. EPA. October 10, 2020. https://epa.com.ng/2020/10/10/its-not-about-sars-by-fr-prof-anthony-akinwale/.

Chapter 9: The Yeast

1. Cousin, J.. "Diocletian." Encyclopedia Britannica, February 27, 2024. https://www.britannica.com/biography/Diocletian.

2. "Diocletian, Persecution of | Encyclopedia.com." n.d. www.

encyclopedia.com. https://www.encyclopedia.com/religion/
encyclopedias-almanacs-transcripts-and-maps/diocletian-per-
secution.

3. "The Tenth Persecution, under Diocletian, A.D. 303 - Fox's
    Book of Martyrs." n.d. Biblestudytools.com. https://
    www.biblestudytools.com/history/foxs-book-of-martyrs/
    the-tenth-persecution-under-diocletian-a-d-303.html.

4. Cavendish, Richard. 2005. "Abdication of the Emperor Dio-
    cletian | History Today." www.historytoday.com. May 5, 2005.
    https://www.historytoday.com/archive/abdication-emper-
    or-diocletian.

5. Cavendish, Richard. 2012. "The Battle of the Milvian Bridge
    | History Today." n.d. www.historytoday.com. https://www.
    historytoday.com/archive/battle-milvian-bridge#:~:tex-
    t=That%20night%20Constantine%20had%20a.

6. Lippold, A.. "Theodosius I." Encyclopedia Britannica, January
    13, 2024. https://www.britannica.com/biography/Theodo-
    sius-I.

Chapter 10: The Shrewd Steward

1. Kevin. "Jim Elliot's Journal Entry with 'He Is No Fool...'
    Quote: Anchored in Christ." Anchored in Christ | KevinHal-
    loran.net, April 14, 2023. https://www.kevinhalloran.net/jim-
    elliot-quote-he-is-no-fool/.

2. Henry, Matthew. *The Complete Works of the rev. Matthew Henry:
    (his unfinished commentary excepted) being a collection of all his treatises,
    sermons, and tracts, as published by himself, and a memoir of his life.*
    Grand Rapids, MI: Baker Book House, 1979.

Chapter 11: The Pearl and the Hidden Treasure

1. Ritchie, Hannah, Lucas Rodés-Guirao, Edouard Mathieu, Mar-
    cel Gerber, Esteban Ortiz-Ospina, Joe Hasell, and Max Ros-
    er. "Population Growth." Our World in Data, July 11, 2023.

Accessed February 27, 2024. https://ourworldindata.org/population-growth.

2. "Bible Facts." King James Bible Dictionary. Accessed February 29, 2024. https://kingjamesbibledictionary.com/BibleFacts.

By the Same Author

When God Speaks in Parables (Volume 2)

This volume digs deep to reveal the hidden gems in the following powerful parables told by Jesus Christ:

i. The Workers in the Vineyard
ii. The Great Banquet
iii. The Fishing Net
iv. The Wineskin and Cloth
v. The Talents
vi. The Wicked Tenants
vii. The Travelling Owner of the House
viii. The Faithful Servant
ix. The Persistent Widow
x. The Importunate Friend

When God Speaks in Parables (Volume 3)

This volume digs deep to reveal the hidden gems in the following powerful parables told by Jesus Christ:

i. The Rich Fool
ii. The Lost Coin
iii. The Lost Sheep
iv. The Prodigal Son
v. The Unmerciful Servant
vi. The Good Samaritan
vii. The Scribe or the Household Treasure
viii. The Travelling Owner of the House
ix. The Faithful and Evil Servants
x. The Fishing Net

CONTACT THE AUTHOR

To contact the author for prayers, counselling, preaching engagements, or other resources:

Website: www.lovedindeed.com
E-mail: lovedindeed01@gmail.com

Made in the USA
Las Vegas, NV
11 November 2024

11626223R00109